# Is a Flight Attendant Career Right for You?

## JOSEPH BELOTTI

Copyright © 1998 - 2018

Orion Communications. Reproduction Strictly Prohibited.

Questions or Comments? Email us: support@airlinecareer.com or visit our website: http://airlinecareer.com. Product names, brands, and other trademarks referred to within this book are the property of their respective trademark holders. Unless otherwise specified, no association between the author and any trademark holder is expressed or implied. Use of a term in this book should not be regarded as affecting the validity of any trademark, registered trademark, or service mark.

ISBN 9781980232919

# TABLE OF CONTENTS

| | | |
|---|---|---|
| 1 | Introduction | 1 |
| 2 | Minimum Qualifications | 9 |
| 3 | Labor Unions | 18 |
| 4 | Scheduling and Job Flexibility | 23 |
| 5 | How Much Can I Earn? | 38 |
| 6 | Benefits | 47 |
| 7 | Duties and Responsibilities | 58 |
| 8 | Domiciles and Relocation | 72 |
| 9 | Management Opportunities | 80 |
| 10 | Fear Factors | 85 |
| | Useful Links | 91 |
| | Appendix | 93 |
| | About the Author | 102 |
| | About the Publisher | 103 |
| | Final Thoughts | 104 |

# 1 INTRODUCTION

So, you *want* to become a flight attendant. Or, more specifically, you *think* you want to become a flight attendant. Most aspiring flight attendants are eager to jump right into the application process without first thoroughly researching the career. Do not make this mistake! Do your due diligence and research the career *first* by reading this book cover to cover. We guarantee you will find a host of invaluable information - both positive and negative - that will allow you to make an informed career decision. Understanding what you are getting yourself into could potentially save you a lot of time and effort, especially if you determine in advance that this career is not for you.

Unfortunately, most of today's applicants know very little about the flight attendant career, basing their desire to work in this industry on myths and stereotypes. Many apply, but few know what the job is all about. Consequently, many new-hires are dissatisfied with the demands of the job and ultimately quit to pursue other professions (this explains the high turnover rate). We do not want this to happen to you.

The last thing you want to do is put the effort into applying for the job and attend 4 to 7 weeks of typically unpaid flight attendant training only to discover *then* that the job does not measure up to your expectations. On the flip side of this, it is our hope that this book will help you discover a real passion for one of the most rewarding, dynamic, and challenging careers in the world.

When you are finished reading this book you should know whether you would like to pursue a flight attendant career. If you are absolutely sure that this job is for you, then you should proceed to read the other books in the "How to Become a Flight Attendant" series which will allow you to delve into the application process and learn critical insider information that will give you a competitive advantage in your quest to become a flight attendant.

**IMPORTANT:** Even if you already know - with absolute certainty - that you want to become a flight attendant, do not skim over this book. This is more than just an evaluation resource; it includes essential information for getting hired, surviving new-hire training and probation, and keeping the job. There is also a great deal of information on how you are paid and how much you can make. Many of the italicized terms referenced in this book can be found in the **"Flight Attendant Dictionary"** on our website which will educate you on the special airline industry terms that you will need to know.

## Then & Now

United Airlines was the first commercial airline to hire a female flight attendant in 1930; her name was Ellen Church. She and seven other single women comprised the "original eight" *stewardesses*. Their primary role was to provide comfort to the traveling public. Minimum qualifications were such that the applicants had to be single, registered nurses. Marriage, pregnancy, or weight gain meant instant job termination and most stewardesses were forced out of the profession by age 32 due to "old age."

Thanks largely to the Civil Rights Act of 1964, airlines can no longer discriminate on the basis of race, sex, age, or marital status. This legislation helped transform the job from a short-term endeavor - strictly for young, single women - to a long-term *career* option for virtually anyone.

In the 1970s and 1980s, there was a large influx of men into the industry, which created the need for a non-gender specific term to describe the position. Hence, the term *flight attendant* was born.

Today, there are over 100,000 flight attendants in the United States; 70% are female and 30% are male (this gender gap, however, is narrowing and it is not uncommon to see all male crews on certain flights). Although it was originally a job for young people, airlines are now accepting many older candidates for the flight attendant position. That, coupled with the fact that many career flight attendants are now working well into their later years, means that the flight attendant workforce is aging. According to The Population Research Bureau, half of all flight attendants are age 45 and older, and nearly 22 percent of them are 55 and older. Over 60% are married and one-third have a college degree (although only a high school diploma is required); common majors include Communications, Business, Spanish and

Teaching. Pay averages around $20,000 for the first year, but senior international flight attendants at a major carrier can earn as much as $100,000 after 20 – 25 years. A recent study by The Bureau of Labor Statistics shows the median annual wage for all flight attendants is $48,500. The median wage is the wage at which half the workers in an occupation earned more than that amount and half earned less. The lowest 10 percent earn less than $26,570, and the highest 10 percent earn more than $78,650. The turnover rate is high (especially among new-hires), but job satisfaction is equally high among those who manage to survive the first year. Average seniority is 15 years.

Successful flight attendants describe themselves as friendly, outgoing, patient, flexible, reliable, and punctual (there is absolutely zero tolerance for being late) - unsuccessful ones as aggressive, temperamental, impatient, and inflexible. Typical concerns include job security ("Is my airline going to downsize or go out of business?"), long hours, and low initial pay.

## Perception vs. Reality

When you see a flight attendant walking through an airport terminal, what is your perception? Do you envision someone who serves a few drinks, chats with amicable passengers, and enjoys frequent layovers in exotic cities?

Historically, the public perception of the career has not matched the reality of the job. Today's flight attendant is very different from the stereotypical "stewardess" portrayed in movies and on television. To a certain extent, some of these myths were born out of the "old days" when stewardesses were elegant nurses who worked on spacious airplanes with relatively few passengers. In 1978, however, airline *deregulation* changed everything. The government no longer controlled fares and route structures as they had in the past. This created bidding wars and turned airlines into cost-cutting machines. Today, it is nothing more than a numbers game where more passengers equal greater revenue. The result: planes are now overcrowded, creating cramped conditions and a culture of hostile passengers. This leaves flight attendants in a rather unenviable position.

These are just a few of the not-so-enticing aspects of the job. As a flight attendant, you must:

- Endure 4 to 7 weeks of typically unpaid initial training, a portion of which takes place on nights and weekends.

- Buy a uniform at a cost of approximately $1,000 (automatic bi-monthly payroll deductions are available to help ease this financial burden).

- Endure a 6 to 12-month probationary period during which you will be under scrutiny and required to report to work at a moment's notice.

- Demonstrate remarkable strength and agility (for example, move a 200+ pound beverage cart through cramped aisles or lift heavy suitcases over passengers' heads into tightly packed overhead compartments).

- Remain courteous and professional despite sometimes abusive passenger behavior.

- React quickly to stressful in-flight medical emergencies.

- Endure occasionally violent air turbulence (sometimes without a seatbelt if assisting passengers).

- Experience short periods away from home (usually from 1 to 3 nights at a time).

- Work long hours (up to 16-hour days; typically, no more than 8 hours in-flight).

- Work many weekends and holidays throughout your career when most of your friends and family have days off.

- Attend mandatory annual recurrent training.

- Work occasionally in the presence of prisoners who are escorted by armed guards to court trials or prisons in other cities.

For friendly, outgoing, and patient individuals who can tolerate these negative aspects of the job, a flight attendant career can be very rewarding. Flight attendants do work hard, but they also enjoy many extraordinary benefits. For example, as a flight attendant, you get:

- A great deal of time off (13 to 17 days off per month; roughly 6 months off per year!), up to 10 days at a time.

- Free or reduced-cost travel benefits for yourself and immediate family, covering air travel, lodging, car-rentals, and cruises.

- A lucrative benefits package, often including health and life insurance, credit union membership, employee stock options, a defined contribution and a 401(k)-retirement plan.

- Unmatched variety - Forget the predictability of 9 to 5 cube life!

- Maximum scheduling flexibility - You are not limited to weekends off like the rest of the world!

- The opportunity to see the world.

- The opportunity to meet new people, including many celebrities.

- Independence.

- Responsibility.

- A sense of pride and accomplishment (especially when you help an unaccompanied minor or handicapped passenger safely reach their destination).

## The #1 Priority: Passenger Safety

Many people have lost sight of the fact that flight attendants are onboard an aircraft for one primary reason: passenger safety. Did you know that every U.S. flight attendant crew can complete an entire passenger evacuation in less than 90 seconds? (every new-hire must accomplish this feat during initial training). Furthermore, flight attendants are required by law to be fully trained on safety for every type of aircraft in an airline's fleet.

Indeed, flight attendants are much more than waitresses in the sky. Flight attendants know how to manage and prepare hundreds of passengers and crew in the event of catastrophic events, such as hijackings and land/sea disasters. They know how to fight fires, operate and troubleshoot the oxygen system, open emergency exits, care for the sick, apprehend unruly passengers - even apply first aid and administer CPR.

A perfect example of flight attendants stepping up in the event of an emergency occurred on January 15, 2009. US Airways Flight 1549, an Airbus A320, in the climbout after takeoff from New York City's LaGuardia Airport, struck a flock of Canadian geese just northeast of the George Washington Bridge and consequently lost all engine power. Unable to reach any airport, pilots **Chesley Sullenberger** and **Jeffrey Skiles** glided the plane to a ditching in the Hudson River off Midtown Manhattan. Under the leadership of Captain Sullenberger, all three flight attendants, **Donna Dent** and her colleagues **Sheila Dail** and **Doreen Welsh**, **US Airways** veterans, with a combined flying experience of more than 95 years were able to evacuate all 155 people aboard. All were rescued by nearby boats and there were few serious injuries. The event later became known as "The Miracle on the Hudson."

# 2 MINIMUM QUALIFICATIONS

## Am I Qualified?

One of the first steps in evaluating a flight attendant career is determining whether you qualify for the position. Every airline has a set of minimum hiring requirements.

**IMPORTANT:** Be sure to visit the websites of airlines that interest you to get a current listing of specific minimum hiring requirements for each airline which may differ slightly from the requirements we discuss below.

So how important are these minimum requirements? They are critical to your future as a flight attendant. If you do not meet the minimum hiring requirements (especially in the areas of age, height, education, and citizenship) for a particular airline, you are not qualified for the job. Keep in mind, however, these are only minimum requirements.

To truly separate yourself from the competition and improve your chances of getting hired, you must have something more to offer, such as solid customer service experience, a higher education, excellent communication skills, or the ability to speak a second language. Most airlines use a weighting system, assigning you a score based on your level of qualification; this score then determines whether you will advance in the application process.

**If you are certain you do not meet the minimum hiring requirements for a particular airline, do not bother applying (until you do), since you won't even make it past the first interview.**

# Age

Age is a firm requirement. You either meet the minimum age requirement or you do not. Airlines won't waiver on this. The minimum allowable age for some U.S. airlines is 18, but most require you to be at least 20.

**The age requirement is usually based on the age you will be upon graduation from training**. So, if you are not at the minimum age at the time of your initial application, but will reach that age during training, you can still apply for the job.

With the airline hiring boom now underway, airlines are constantly lowering their minimum age requirements in order to broaden their audience of prospective applicants. We will notify you of changes on a regular basis in our blog.

If you do not meet the minimum age requirement for a particular airline, you can still apply for another position within the airline as a reservationist or customer service agent, which usually have lower minimum age requirements. As an employee of the airline, you would greatly improve your chances of getting hired in the future since most airlines prefer to hire from within rather than take chances on unproven newcomers.

You could also spend this time improving your chances of becoming a flight attendant by taking enrichment courses (such as learning a second language) or getting experience in customer service outside of the airline industry. Customer service experience can be as complex as working as a Dell Technical Support Representative or as simple as working the drive-thru window at Taco Bell. It all counts.

Due to discrimination issues, there are no maximum age requirements. In fact, in every flight attendant class, there is always a small percentage of "older" new-hires. Because there is no age limit, many people are pursuing second careers as flight attendants - and are gladly accepted because of their experience and level of maturity. Do not ever think you are too old to apply for a flight attendant position. A recent class of 100 new hires at a major airline had 7 people between the ages of 40 and 49, 5 people between the ages of 50 and 59, and 1 person over 60!

## Height

Most flight attendants are between 5'2" and 5'9" tall. Outside of this *normal* range, certain airlines have minimum and maximum height requirements.

A very short person may have difficulty reaching the overhead compartments in an airplane, which are typically between 6' and 6'10" inches high. **Some airlines have no minimum height requirement, but do require you to pass a *reach test*.** The reach test is nothing more than a demonstration of your ability to reach all the necessary components inside an airplane's cabin.

 You can perform a reach test on your own. Simply grab a tape measure, measure out a distance of 6'10" from the floor, and mark it on the wall. If you can reach the mark in bare feet, chances are you will pass any airline's reach test.

If you find you do not meet the minimum height requirement for any of the major airlines, do not let this discourage you. You can always apply to be a flight attendant for a small regional airline; commuter and regional jet aircraft are much smaller, making height less critical.

Conversely, if you are a little on the tall side, some airlines' maximum height requirement is right around 6'2". If you are taller than 6'2", keep in mind that you will be working in small *galleys* and may find it difficult to work 8-hour days in such a cramped environment.

## Weight and Health

Airlines used to have stringent height-to-weight guidelines; however, due to a number of recent discrimination lawsuits, most airlines are simply looking for your **height and weight to be proportional**.

Today, it is more important to be in **good shape** than to look like a super model. Airlines need people with the necessary strength to open emergency doors, the agility to attend to passengers in sometimes cramped working conditions, and the stamina to survive 16-hour days. An overweight or out-of-shape person may not have the necessary strength, agility or stamina to perform. We recommend getting yourself into good physical shape before initial training.

The airlines also want healthy people. You will be in contact with thousands of passengers each week, both in the airport and in small airplane cabins (most with recycled air). You will need a strong immune system to ward off illness and a healthy body to bounce back from sometimes grueling 4-day trips. A history of personal illness, drug or alcohol abuse, or a bad family medical history could dissuade certain airlines from hiring you.

All airlines are required by law to administer comprehensive physicals to new-hires. Before applying, make sure you are in good health and drug-free. If you do not pass the physical, you will probably be dismissed by the airline.

**If you have a known, uncorrected problem with your eyesight, see a doctor before the airline's medical exam. During the exam, you will undergo an eye test in which you must demonstrate 20/20 vision, either naturally or with corrective lenses.**

## Education

Virtually every airline requires that you have a high school degree or Government Equivalency Degree (G.E.D.) If you did not finish high school or have not passed the G.E.D., do not bother to apply for a job as a flight attendant. You absolutely won't get hired if you don't possess a minimum of a high school degree (or equivalent).

When you review each airline's minimum hiring qualifications, you should realize that these are merely *minimums*. More is always better, especially when it comes to education. Just because you have a high school degree, do not expect to walk into an airline employment office, show your diploma and get hired. Many airlines look favorably upon applicants who have tried to better themselves by pursuing higher education. A recent study shows that over one-half of all flight attendants hired have at least one year of college under their belt, and over one-third have an Associate's or Bachelor's degree. A few even have Master's degrees or Doctorate's; these types of advanced degrees are certainly not required for the job, but will be helpful if you plan on pursuing a management or supervisory position someday.

Additionally, if you are lacking customer service experience, many airlines will overlook this "weakness" if you have a college education behind you. Hiring departments believe that college experience makes applicants more mature and better able to handle the many challenges and responsibilities that come with being a flight attendant.

## Customer Service Experience

Customer service experience is typically not a firm requirement; meaning, you can usually apply without it. However, a lack of customer service experience makes getting hired that much more difficult. Customer service experience will give you a clear competitive advantage in your quest to become a flight attendant. Remember that you will be working in front of the public on a regular basis. From greeting, serving and assisting passengers to making announcements, you will always be representing the company in a customer service role. Because it is very important to **project a** positive image, airlines are very careful about selecting candidates who have some sort of customer service experience working with the general public. **Most people do not even realize that they have a customer service background.** If you have ever worked in an environment in which you had to deal with the public on a regular basis, you have customer service experience. This can include working in a retail clothing store, waiting tables in a restaurant, answering telephones in a corporate environment, etc.

However, if you do not have any customer service experience, you should not despair. You may have a more difficult time than others who do, but it won't preclude you from landing the job, especially if you excel in other qualification areas. For example, the airlines will usually substitute a college education (even without a degree) for a lack of customer service experience.

 **When it comes time to apply, make sure you have at least some customer service experience or a college education (at least 2 years) behind you. Airlines look very favorably upon such experience.**

## Language Skills

Fluency in a second language, such as French, Spanish, German, Japanese, or Chinese is a major plus in the eyes of flight attendant hiring departments; however, most airlines are only concerned with your ability to speak English. Fluency in English is a must. If you cannot speak English effectively, you won't get hired by a U.S. airline.

Very few airlines require you to be able to speak a second language. Airlines that have a second language preference do so because of certain international destinations. On these routes, a designated *Language of Destination/Origin* (also called *LOD/O* - pronounced "low-doe") flight attendant is assigned to the flight. Such positions are usually awarded to senior flight attendants, making these jobs difficult to obtain even for qualified applicants. Pay is also higher for LOD/O qualified flight attendants - approximately $1.50 to $2.00 higher per hour.

 **Be sure not to exaggerate your ability to speak a foreign language. The airlines will test you to determine your level of fluency.**

## Citizenship

Every major U.S. airline requires you to be a U.S. Citizen or registered alien with legal right to accept employment in the U.S., plus the right to travel to and from the countries the airline serves.

You are also required to have a social security card and, in many instances, a passport. If you do not have a passport, it might be a good idea to get one now by visiting the US Department of State at https://Travel.State.gov. They take just a few weeks to obtain.

## Relocation

Every major airline requires that you be willing to relocate to any of the listed flight attendant domiciles.

## Appearance

The airlines are very particular about hiring individuals who have a neat and attractive appearance. After all, flight attendants are the only employees to have direct, continuous contact with the traveling public. No matter what the marketing department propagates over the airwaves or in print, flight attendants must look neat and professional in order for the airline to develop an appealing brand identity.

Typically, airlines do not permit visible tattoos, body piercings (save for your ears), long hair on men, "rebellious" hairstyles, bizarre or offensive-looking makeup or jewelry, poorly manicured hands, etc. All airlines are different. For example, some do not even permit facial hair on men! During training, you will be given specific grooming regulations which must be strictly adhered to.

## Company Physical and Background Check

If you have thoroughly read through the minimum hiring requirements (above), you may be thinking it would be easy enough to "cheat" a little bit during the application process - maybe say you are a year older or an inch taller than you actually are, or fail to mention that DWI conviction you had three years ago. You do not want to do this, trust us!

Airlines have a couple of ways to determine whether applicants have lied on their application about their age, height, past use of drugs, work history, or any other area that would preclude them from landing the job.

Every airline administers a company physical examination to every new-hire. During this exam, an airline can detect whether you lied on your application about your height, whether you have a drug or alcohol problem, or whether your past medical history shows anything adverse that would disqualify you from getting the job. Since you are given a urinalysis during this physical, it is very important that you inform the examiners of any medications you might be taking.

In addition to the medical exam, there is also a thorough background check. During the background check, which can go back as many as 10 years, virtually everything about you is investigated - your age, place of birth, school records, criminal records (if any), etc. **If an airline finds that you lied on your application or you have any sort of criminal record, you will be immediately dismissed.**

# 3 LABOR UNIONS

## The Role of the Union

Upon completion of the 6 to 12-month probationary period, you will be required to join a flight attendant labor union (i.e., if your airline has one). You will have to pay monthly union dues (typically around $40 to $60), but it is certainly worth the investment. The union continually seeks to improve members' wages, hours, benefits, working conditions, and job security. Major functions include negotiating labor contracts and handling job disputes. Unions also actively represent flight attendants in the media and fight battles in the political arena.

Some airlines do not have a flight attendant labor union, in which case, the company is able to dictate pay scales, benefits, working conditions, etc. Non-union airlines typically offer less job security and lower pay and benefits. An exception to this is Delta Airlines. Delta does not have a flight attendant union, but offers a labor package that is highly competitive with its unionized counterparts.

## Major Flight Attendant Unions

The largest flight attendant union in the U.S. is the **Association of Flight Attendants (AFA-CWA)**, representing 47,000 flight attendants from 26 airlines. Besides the AFA, there are 4 other unions, many of which extend membership to pilots and mechanics: **International Brotherhood of Teamsters (IBT), Transport Workers Union of America (TWU), International Association of Machinists (IAM), and Association of Professional Flight Attendants (APFA).** We urge you to visit the union web sites for more information.

## Contract Negotiations

Every 3 to 5 years, a new flight attendant working agreement must be renegotiated between union representatives and airline management. The working agreement covers pay, benefits, union security, seniority, scheduling, work rules, vacation, sick time, the handling of grievances (complaints), etc.

Union goals always differ from the goals of airline management. Management seeks to maximize profits through cost-cutting measures, while the union seeks higher wages and improved benefits for its members. The two sides settle their differences and establish conditions that are mutually acceptable through a process called *collective bargaining*.

In a typical bargaining session, representatives of the flight attendant negotiating committee make demands. Management responds by making a counteroffer that meets some, but not all, of the union's demands. The two sides then try to work out a compromise.

Usually contract talks begin several months before the existing agreement comes to an end and can last for several months - in some cases, past the expiration date of the previous contract.

Most disputes between unions and management involve pay and working conditions. If labor and management cannot settle their differences, they may receive outside help (called *mediation*). If the two sides still cannot agree, they may submit to a process called *arbitration*. A person called an *arbitrator* hears the evidence and hands down a decision that is binding on both sides.

## Strikes

Unless it has a no-strike agreement, a union may call a strike to press its demands at any time during a dispute with management. Strikes occur when workers feel such action is the best way to pressure management into meeting their demands. Before a union calls a strike, it must put the question to a vote by its members (only those members employed by the particular airline, not the whole union). In most unions, a strike cannot be called unless a majority of those voting support such action.

In a typical strike, flight attendants organize into small groups and form picket lines in highly visible areas. The pickets try to prevent other employees from working and the public from doing business with the airline. Strikers who cross the picket line to work are called *scabs*.

Many strikes succeed during periods of low unemployment and prosperous economic conditions. During periods of less prosperity and high unemployment, more strikes fail. Workers can hardly afford the loss of income and may return to work without winning any of their demands.

There have been some very lengthy strikes in aviation history. During the Eastern Airlines strike of the late 80s, airline management refused to succumb to labor's demands, and it ultimately caused the demise of the airline. In the mid-80s, during a lengthy Continental Airlines strike, many pilots were faced with the ultimatum of giving in to management and returning to work or losing their jobs. Although some pilots eventually returned, many lost their jobs to pilots hired from outside the airline.

Strikes can cost an airline several million dollars a day. Very often, management personnel are used as temporary replacements, but the airline is still usually forced to cancel many flights.

During a long walkout, you can be without pay for sometimes several months. And at the end of the strike, depending on its severity, the airline may elect to cut its work force (including you), *furloughing* employees in reverse order of seniority - to save money.

Strikes, or work stoppages, are a very real part of the airline business and should be considered when evaluating this profession.

## C.H.A.O.S.

CHAOS is a form of work stoppage that has been used in the past and is a trademark of the AFA-CWU union. The term CHAOS is an acronym for **C**reate **H**avoc **A**round **O**ur **S**ystem. During CHAOS, flight attendants are instructed by their union to walk off selected flights, thereby causing schedule disruptions and possible flight cancellations.

CHAOS has been tested by several flight attendant unions. For example, in April 2000, US Airways was able to reach a working agreement with airline management by threatening CHAOS. US Airways management threatened to shut down the airline rather than subject its passengers to CHAOS, but an agreement was reached just prior to the union's published deadline. This type of stoppage has not been used in recent years, but other forms of work stoppages under different names have caused service interruptions and have been effective in reaching agreements with airline managements.

# 4 SCHEDULING AND JOB FLEXIBILITY

## Flight Hours

One of the most common questions people ask flight attendants is "How much do you work?" The short answer is 70 to 85 hours per month, as compared to the typical 9 to 5er who works 160 hours per month. But before you click over to the Application Center in pursuit of this dream job, you must understand that these figures are very misleading.

As a flight attendant, your livelihood is based on *flight hours*. You earn flight hours from the time an aircraft pushes back from the gate to the time it arrives at the gate of your destination. The more flight hours you accumulate over the course of a month, the greater your pay. In this sense, a flight attendant does indeed work 70 to 85 hours per month, but these are merely flight hours. These figures do not account for the time you will spend during pre-flight, boarding, deplaning, driving to and from the airport, or sleeping in a hotel room. If you take all of these factors into consideration, your total monthly work time jumps to between 250 and 300 hours!

**Flight attendants commonly refer to flight hours as block time. The reason: blocks are removed from beneath an aircraft's tires just prior to pushback; they are repositioned following arrival. Because of this procedure, airline crewmembers are said to work** *block-to-block.*

## Lineholders

Flight attendants come in two varieties: lineholders and reserves. Lineholders are at the top of the flight attendant hierarchy. They are employees - typically senior ones - who have earned the right to hold a *regular line of time*.

In laymen's terms, a line of time is nothing more than a schedule. Regular lines of time are created by each airline and consist of detailed flight pairings over a 4-week period. Each line of time is unique. The aircraft, flight hours, the number of days off, the frequency of trips, the times of day/week worked, the cities of destination, etc. can vary tremendously. As a result, certain lines of time are more desirable than others.

Lineholders get to bid on their preferred lines of time each month. They are ultimately awarded a single line of time that lets them know specifically what trips they will be flying, when they will be flying them, and which days they will have off - over a 4-week period. **The key here from a scheduling standpoint is that, as a lineholder, you**

**get to pick your trips <u>and</u> have advanced knowledge of your entire schedule for the month.**

In a large base, you may have 250 lines of time to choose from for your monthly schedule. Each month, these lines are distributed in a *bid package*; they are also commonly available on the Internet. The airline publishes these lines with an opening and closing date for bidding purposes. Similar to an auction, you bid on lines that suit your needs. That is, you specify the flights you wish to work in order of preference.

Unlike an auction that uses cash for bidding purposes, you use your seniority number to get the line you want. The person with the highest seniority gets first choice, the person with the next highest seniority gets second choice, and so on down the line until all trips are awarded.

As a lineholder, you get to enjoy maximum scheduling flexibility. You can choose your preferred monthly schedule based on any number of factors, including:

- **Cities of destination** - Perhaps you have friends in Los Angeles? You could choose a monthly schedule that has long, frequent *layovers* in LAX. Ideally, you would want a lengthy RON in LAX; RON stands for Remain Overnight.
- **Consecutive days off** - Want to create a simulated "vacation" for yourself? You could choose a line of time that calls for hard work at the beginning and end of the month, but enjoy 10 consecutive days off to relax, travel, etc. in the middle of the month. There are not too many jobs that offer this kind of flexibility.
- **Time of day/week** - Many flight attendants operate small businesses out of their homes selling real estate or building web sites. If you are the entrepreneurial type, you could try to

fly nights and weekends in order to free up your valuable weekdays for meetings with clients. Maybe you are a student, an actor, or a musician? You could choose a schedule that meets your specific needs. Of course, you will need high seniority to afford yourself the luxury of guaranteed days off.

- **Time away from home** - Perhaps you want to spend more time with your children or pets? You could bid for lines of times that call for more frequent, shorter trips, thus limiting your time away from home. *Turnarounds*, trips that depart and return on the same day with no overnight stay, would probably be most desirable.
- **Crewmembers** - Many flight attendants, especially married couples, enjoy working together. Through a process called *buddy bidding*, certain airlines permit you to fly a monthly line of time with another flight attendant (assuming you have sufficient seniority). This means you could work the exact same schedule for a month with your best friend, husband/wife, etc. This obviously makes working a lot more enjoyable.

Even after the bid has closed, some airlines will let you make adjustments to your schedule. For example, you can drop your own trips, pick up others that are in *open time* (trips that have not been assigned or have been dropped by another flight attendant), or even trade trips with other flight attendants who are willing to do so.

You do not control your own destiny in the bidding process. While you have the potential to have a great schedule each and every month, you are at the mercy of your seniority number. If other more senior flight attendants are awarded

IS A FLIGHT ATTENDANT CAREER RIGHT FOR YOU?

**your preferred lines of time, you will have to settle for less appealing alternatives.**

As a lineholder, all of this flexibility is tempered by certain restrictions. All flight attendants must abide by Federal Aviation Regulations (also called FARs - pronounced "F-A-Rs") and contractual work rules.

FARs deal with everything from on-board emergency procedures to alcohol and drug policies for crewmembers. Specific work-related FARs exist to protect flight attendants from overwork and the traveling public from poor service. The FAA limits the number of hours you can work each day, week, month, and year. For example, the daily maximum on-duty period is 16 hours. Anything beyond 16 hours is illegal. Actual flight time is limited to 8 hours. The FAA also requires minimum rest periods between trips.

Besides the FARs, there are also airline-specific contractual work rules, which are negotiated by the flight attendant union. In most cases, the rules provided in your flight attendant labor contract are more stringent than those provided by the FAA. For example, most flight attendant contracts allow a maximum daily on-duty period of 14 hours, rather than the FAA's 16 hours. **Neither the FARs nor the contractual work rules may be violated, otherwise you can expect a fine, termination, or both.**

Mechanical problems and bad weather can wreak havoc on your monthly line of time. In these situations, you may spend countless hours at the airport waiting for a situation to be resolved and become *illegal* (i.e., reach the contractual daily work limit) long before your workday is scheduled to end. In these instances, you will be *grounded*, reserves will be called in to complete the trip, and your planned **RON** in **LAX** will become a mere fantasy.

Because of the above-mentioned rules and regulations, an airline must build your monthly line of time based on the government mandated and company contractual guidelines. As mentioned, these are built-in protections that prevent you from working unreasonable hours or too many days in one month. Most major airlines permit you to fly a maximum of 85 hours per month. And since most flight attendants want to earn as much money as possible each month, they will typically work what is called a *full month*. When you work a full month, you have flown the maximum number of flight hours allowed by the airline for the month. Sometimes you are awarded a line of time that falls short of the airline's flight hour maximum. In this case, you will need to pick up extra trips in order to "get your time in."

Conversely, some flight attendants, especially students and those with families, attempt to fly as little as possible each month, maximizing their time off (but also limiting their pay). Because of this, airlines also impose flight hour minimums as part of their contractual work rules; however, at certain airlines, *line sharing* is permitted, giving a flight attendant the option of splitting his or her schedule with another flight attendant. Some airlines also offer monthly *flight hour option* programs for lineholders in which they are only required to fly 50 or 75 hours in a given month - rather than the usual 80 or 85. Of course, pay is also reduced. These individuals are usually senior flight attendants who have other interests outside of the airline and need the extra time off in order to run a business, take care of growing children, or just want to maintain a reduced schedule in their later years. This a very appealing aspect of the job, since very few companies (outside the airline industry) allow full-time employees to work just 8 to 10 days a month.

Go to The Appendix to see an example of a **Regular Line of Time.**

 All this talk about flight hours can make your head spin. If you want to estimate the total number of days per month you can expect to work as a flight attendant, consider the following: If you are only allowed to fly a maximum of 85 hours per month and you manage to average 5 to 6 flight hours per day worked, it will take you 14 to 17 days to get your time in.

## Reserves

Everyone wants to be a lineholder. After all, you get to bid on and receive a relatively stable schedule each month. But all airlines need reserves, flight attendants who are ready to fill-in at a moment's notice when lineholders become sick, illegal, or are otherwise unable to work.

Like lineholders, reserves bid on monthly lines of time; however, their lines of time are much more limited. While a reserve schedule does include very specific days off (usually 11 days per month, during which you are 100% off-duty and free to do as you please), the remainder of the month is a complete mystery. That is to say, you are simply *on-duty*, round-the-clock, with no schedule whatsoever - save for the fact you are on-duty.

When you are on-duty (roughly 19 days per month), you are said to be *on call*. Though you are not actually working, you have to be ready to fly at a moment's notice. Your bags must be packed, your uniform pressed, and your car full of gas. Crew scheduling will contact you via telephone *if they need you*. This means staying in your house or apartment all day waiting for a telephone call that may never come. Of course, you can give yourself increased freedom by purchasing a cell phone (at your own expense). But cell phones are not fault-proof, and if crew scheduling fails to reach you (they will usually try to contact you for up to 10 minutes), you will receive a *no-contact* infraction, which is grounds for termination.

 **Should you choose to leave your home or apartment on your on-duty days, you will want to exercise caution, since you will typically have no more than 20 minutes to get home, get dressed, and hit the road.**

Most airlines require you to live (i.e., maintain a permanent address and telephone number) within 1 hour of your domicile. If your primary residence does not qualify (and you do not want to move), you will probably want to share a small apartment or hotel room in close proximity to the airport with several other flight attendants during your on-duty days. This is commonly referred to as a *crash pad*. The more flight attendants involved, the lower the cost for everyone.

Typically, reserves are new-hires; however, even many veteran flight attendants are not senior enough to hold regular lines of time at certain domiciles. Some airlines even rotate reserves and lineholders throughout the year, regardless of seniority. The average flight attendant "sits" reserve for a period of 2 to 10 years. You can accelerate this process by relocating to a *junior* domicile or choosing an airline that is in an active hiring mode.

 **During on-duty periods, you may not work at all if the airline does not need you. Fortunately, the airlines have something called a monthly minimum guarantee for reserves. This means you will receive a guaranteed minimum amount** of money even if you do not accrue a single flight hour. On the flip side of this, you can work so much in a given month that you

actually become illegal. In these instances, you are no longer legally available to fly, meaning you get to enjoy the rest of the month off - regardless of your on/off-duty reserve schedule.

Go to the Appendix to see a **Reserve Line of Time.**

# Probation

During your first year of employment, you will be required to complete a probationary period, ranging from 6 months to a year.

As a *reserve on probation*, you must be on your best behavior and strive to perform your duties in the best possible manner. Every move you make will be analyzed by everyone around you, from the captain on down to the flight attendants and ticket agents. You will be evaluated in all areas of job performance, attendance and dependability, overall attitude, and adherence to uniform and grooming guidelines.

Because of the many stresses associated with the probationary period, many new-hires quit to pursue other careers. Consider the following and determine if you have what it takes to survive probation:

- You will likely have to relocate to an unfamiliar city.
- You will likely work every holiday and weekend when most of your friends and family will want to get together.
- You won't have a predictable schedule that will allow you to watch your favorite television shows every night and cuddle up with your dog.
- You won't be able to drink alcoholic beverages during your on-duty days - roughly 19 days per month. The FARs prohibit crewmembers from drinking alcoholic beverages

within 8 hours of working - and most airlines' drinking policies are even more stringent.
- You won't be able to show up late to work and get away with it. There is zero tolerance for tardiness in this profession, especially during probation.

To be a successful new-hire, you must be incredibly flexible, willing to tolerate a hectic and uncertain lifestyle. But remember, you are simply paying your dues. Over time, you will gain enough seniority to become a lineholder and get to enjoy one of the greatest careers in the world.

## RONs

For many flight attendants, especially new-hires, the RON (pronounced "R-O-N"), which stands for Remain Overnight, is one of the most appealing aspects of the job. It is a unique feature of the monthly schedule that allows crewmembers to tour, shop, and socialize in various parts of the country - and world. For others, however, especially the more senior flight attendants with families, the RON is a curse; they will usually try to bid short stays away from home as well as day trips to avoid staying in a hotel room overnight.

The RON is what you make of it. Some are long and enjoyable ways to relax and explore the sights and sounds of a new city. Others are so short you may not even remember staying overnight at all. In some instances, you may work a 16-hour day only to spend less than 10 hours on the ground before your next flight in the morning; by the time you get to the hotel and get to bed, you will be lucky to get 6 or 7 hours of sleep! Unfortunately, for new-hires, these types of RONs are the norm, while the longer more exotic ones are usually flown by more senior flight attendants.

## IS A FLIGHT ATTENDANT CAREER RIGHT FOR YOU?

During RONs, crewmembers usually go out to dinner together or frequent a local pub for a relaxing cocktail. Unfortunately, some new-hires make the mistake of overindulging and unwind to the point of embarrassment. Although you are technically off-duty on a RON, it is important to maintain a level of professionalism. After all, you are always under the watchful eyes of the captain and crew, and any socially deviant behavior may be reported to your supervisor.

Generally, on a short layover, you won't leave your room; instead, you will go straight to bed. Although you probably won't get yourself into social trouble on this type of RON, there is still a potential pitfall: being late for the van. Upon check-in at the hotel, while picking up your room key, one of the pilots or senior flight attendant will tell you *precisely* what time to be downstairs in the lobby the next morning. It is okay to be early, but never be late; 5:00 A.M. means 5:00 A.M., not 5:05 A.M. If the van leaves without you, you will be held accountable, and your job will be on the line.

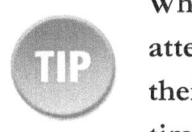

**What time is it, anyway? Most domestic flight attendants make it a policy to stay on the time zone of their home base to avoid any confusion as to what time it really is. Always ask what the van time is for your own time zone and ignore the local time. Of course, if you are flying international trips with a multi-day RON, this may not be possible.**

A crewmember's worst nightmare is not waking up in time to catch the van. Imagine getting a phone call from the captain telling you the crew is waiting downstairs and you have not even gotten out of bed! Should this ever happen to you, you will have to bypass the shower and work, perhaps a long day, feeling like you just rolled out of bed (literally).

 During RONs, most conscientious crewmembers set two alarms plus ask for a wake-up call from the hotel. But do not rely exclusively on the hotel to wake you up; they are notorious for forgetting, or calling the wrong room. Invest in a good alarm clock (or two) that is wind up or battery operated or just use the alarm on your cell phone. Do not rely on hotel power, because sometimes the power will go out for a few minutes while you are asleep and you will wake to a flashing 12:00!

## Crew Schedulers

Behind-the-scenes, daily and central crew schedulers work tirelessly to manage the day-to-day drama of flight operations.

Daily crew schedulers are under constant pressure to make sure flights depart on-time with a sufficient number of legal crewmembers. They must move quickly in the event that a crewmember fails to make check-in (or calls in sick) by making the dreaded *quick call* to an on-duty reserve. All the while, they must determine which flight attendants are available to work considering vacations, days off, flight hour limits, etc.

The central crew schedulers have the unenviable task of trying to restore an airline to normal operation during times of severe weather, mechanicals, and ATC (Air Traffic Control) delays.

Most reserves are very familiar with their crew schedulers. After all, they are the ones who wake you in the middle of the night and say, "We need you here in 20 minutes." While many new-hires fear the "villainous" voice of crew scheduling, truth be told, they can be your best friend or your worst enemy. They are your best friend when they assign you an "easy" 2-day with a RON in PHX; they are your worst enemy when they sentence you to a brutal 4-day that culminates with a LAX to BOS *red-eye* - and the last leg requires you to *deadhead* (fly as a passenger) home.

You will come to know many of their names at the smaller airlines. But at the larger ones, you may never speak directly to a human crew scheduler. More and more airlines are opting for fully computerized scheduling systems, so do not be surprised if a computer contacts you for your first quick call.

## Supervisors

Every flight attendant is assigned a specific flight attendant supervisor. This person serves as your boss and keeps a very close eye on you throughout your probationary period. Should you ever violate one of the FARs or contractual work rules, you will have to answer to your supervisor; this can be anything from wearing an unauthorized uniform accessory to a no-contact infraction.

During probation, supervisors will give you surprise evaluation rides, uniform checks, and performance critiques. It is important that you impress your supervisor, but be careful not to become so preoccupied with impressing him or her that you fail to do your job effectively.

## Seniority

Today, most people in corporate America are rewarded with raises, job promotions and bonuses based on merit; if you do an outstanding job, you will move up the corporate ladder. For a flight attendant, however, things are very different.

Every flight attendant is expected to perform at a high level. If you manage to stand head-and-shoulders above your peers, you might get a complimentary letter in your file, or you could be offered a job as a flight attendant supervisor - but nothing more.

Everything you do throughout your entire career revolves around seniority, your numerical ranking within the flight attendant hierarchy. This number, which is published in a seniority list, is usually based on your date of hire or, in some cases, the date you completed new hire training.

Your seniority number essentially controls your life. From the day you are hired, it determines your base assignment, schedule, vacation, pass privileges, pay, and overall working conditions. But rest assured, if you do your job, your seniority will improve over time.

**When choosing an airline, make sure you choose one that is in an active hiring mode. Your seniority will increase more rapidly if an abundant number of flight attendants is hired after you have been hired. If you join an airline that is on the brink of a hiring freeze or layoffs, your seniority will suffer. This means you will be stuck sitting reserve for a longer period of time than necessary. Your only hope to earn a regular line of time would be waiting for more senior flight attendants to retire or quit. You should also realize that seniority is airline-specific. If you spend many years gaining seniority at a particular airline, it is not transferable to another airline. If you quit or are the victim of a layoff, you will have to start over from ground zero as a reserve with another airline - so pick your airline very carefully.**

Upon graduation from new-hire training, your initial seniority ranking will probably be based on your age. Since everyone in your class will have the same date of hire, date of birth is often used to break it down even further, with the oldest in the class having the highest seniority number.

# 5 HOW MUCH CAN I EARN?

## The Basics of Compensation

Unlike most 9 to 5 office workers who earn salaries that are privately negotiated and performance-based, flight attendants are paid an hourly union rate that is based almost entirely on seniority. For example, all first-year flight attendants at a particular airline might earn $19 per hour; all sixth-year flight attendants, $32 per hour; and all fourteenth-year flight attendants, $56 per hour. Each airline's hourly *base rate* is unique. Some airlines pay higher hourly rates than others. It all depends on the labor contract. Every 3 to 5 years, each airline negotiates a new labor contract with its flight attendant union. Once compensation is agreed upon, it is fixed for the duration of the contract.

As a flight attendant, you won't be paid this hourly rate for every hour that you work. The time you spend commuting to the airport, sleeping in hotel rooms, standing around the airport between flights, and assisting passengers during boarding and deplaning is essentially unpaid labor. Most airlines only pay you from the time an aircraft pushes back from the gate to the time it arrives at the gate of its destination. This is commonly referred to as *flight time*, *block time*, or *hard time*.

Technically, flight attendants are paid based on accrued *pay time*, which includes block time plus any excess *claim time*. Claim time is time paid in excess of block time. For example, if you were required to deadhead to another city during a trip, you would not work the flight (and would not earn block time), but would be entitled to additional *deadhead time*. This additional time would be reflected in your pay time.

The major exception to this is meal expenses. Most airlines pay a nominal hourly rate to cover meal expenses. Hotel lodging is paid for by the airline.

**Instead of flight time-based pay, certain airlines compensate flight attendants based on the number of accrued monthly flight miles. Others pay flat salaries regardless of the hours (or miles) flown. These compensation methods are unique, but you should nevertheless be aware of them.**

As mentioned above, job performance has virtually no impact on your pay. You are expected to work at a high level and will never receive a bonus or promotion of any kind, even for exemplary service. This may seem a little strange to you, especially if you have spent a portion of your life in an office building trying to climb the corporate ladder. On the positive side, since pay is tied directly to seniority, you will receive guaranteed annual pay raises; they are built right into the contract. As a new-hire, you might even receive a mandatory pay raise after only 6 months of employment, immediately following the probationary period. Another positive aspect of unionized labor is that it eliminates much of the jealousy and biases that surround compensation in corporate America. For example, you will never hear someone say, "I wonder what they are paying him?, or "I know they are not paying me what I'm worth because I'm a minority." After all, seniority determines pay, which cannot be influenced by human prejudices. On the negative side, however, you are essentially at the mercy of the labor contract and have no negotiating power as an individual when it comes to compensation. If you believe you are underpaid, you cannot exactly walk into your supervisor's office and ask for more money. Instead, you must rely on your union representatives to stand up for you - and every other flight attendant who works for the airline - during contract negotiations.

**Since you cannot negotiate pay as a flight attendant, be sure to choose an airline that makes the most financial sense before accepting employment. You will want to choose an airline that is in an active hiring mode. This will help you gain seniority more quickly, resulting in better pay. You should also choose an airline with competitive pay rates. Granted, contracts change every 3 to 5 years, but typically frugal airlines stay frugal and more generous ones stay generous. If you want to make the most amount of money, stick to the major airlines.**

To a certain extent, any flight attendant can simply peruse the labor contract to determine what a fellow employee is earning. After all, if you know someone's date of hire, you can easily determine their hourly rate; it is in the contract! You must realize, however, that although flight hour base rates are fixed, actual monthly income can vary even between flight attendants with comparable seniority. For example, some airlines offer a premium pay rate to flight attendants who work the *lead* or *A flight attendant* position, work at night or on certain weekends and holidays, or fly international flights. Additionally, the number of flight hours a flight attendant chooses to fly in a given month has a dramatic effect on income.

Certain airlines have a two-tiered wage system which also affects how much you can earn as a flight attendant.

## B-Scale and the Two-Tiered Wage System

Back in the mid-80's, with rising labor costs and increasing fuel prices, airline management sought innovative ways to increase their bottom line. Unfortunately, for the airline labor force, one of the biggest changes was the introduction of the *B-scale*. Initially introduced and implemented by American Airlines for its pilots, the B-scale was negotiated with labor unions in exchange for growth. By guaranteeing new hiring and growth within the airline, airline management wanted a second tier of wages for new hires who were essentially doing the same job as other employees. A time limit was established in the contract which determined how long an individual would be required to be on B-scale. At most airlines, *A-scale* wages did not begin until after 5 years of employment - in some cases, even longer. Once the American pilot union accepted the B-scale for its pilots, many employee groups, including flight attendants, shortly followed suit and the concept quickly spread throughout the industry. Today, with newer contracts being negotiated, **many companies are giving up the B-scale** in exchange for other employee concessions, but a few airlines still have some sort of B-scale although it may not be called that.

 If the airline that hires you has a B-scale, you can expect to be on it for at least 5 years. This is another factor to consider when choosing an airline. You will be working alongside flight attendants doing the exact same job as yourself, but they will be making a lot more money.

## Maximizing your Flight Time

In the airline business, you are constantly tracking what is known as your *monthly projection*. If your contract allows you to fly a maximum of 85 hours per month, you are constantly striving to reach this legal limit by month's end. If you reach it, you have earned a full month. Anything less and you are depriving yourself of potential earnings. Crewmembers constantly strive to fly the most number of hours in the fewest number of days, thereby giving themselves more time off for essentially the same money.

Most airlines pay by the flight hour. To determine your monthly pay, it is simply a matter of multiplying your hourly pay rate by the number of hours flown in a given month.

For purposes of explanation, let's imagine a fictitious airline called Orion Airlines. Let's say their contractual hourly base rate for a first-year flight attendant is $19.05 per hour. If you were to fly 85 hours in one month as a first-year flight attendant at Orion Airlines, you would earn:

**$19.05/hr x 85 hrs = $1,619.25** for flight hours flown. This equates to approximately $19,431.00 per year, assuming you were to continue to fly at or near the monthly legal limit for flight hours.

Calculating pay gets a bit more technical in the real world, but for purposes of evaluating this career, it is not necessary to focus on the details.

## Meal Expenses

In addition to base rate earnings for accrued flight hours, flight attendants are also paid a *per diem* rate for meal expenses. Per diem is Latin for "by the day" and is nothing more than a daily meal allowance covering the period from check-in to the end of a trip. Since the airline pays for your hotel directly, this is the only expense allowance you will need while on the road.

During an 85-hour month, your meal expenses can be quite substantial since you could be away from base anywhere from 200 to 300 hours. Let's use the example of Orion Airlines to figure expense money. Let's say Orion Airlines pays you $1.90 for each hour you are away from base. Using this per diem rate, during a month in which you are away from base for 250 hours, you would earn:

**$1.90/hr x 250 hrs = $475.00** for meal expenses.

During that same 85-hour month, you would earn $1,619.25 (base pay). This adds up to $2,094.25. **If you maintained this schedule for 12 months, this would give you an annual income of $25,131.** Since many airlines provide crew meals and extra passenger meals to flight attendants at no cost while working, per diem is usually more than enough to cover meal expenses. After all, sometimes you are only buying 1 or 2 meals (or snacks) per day.

 **Most flight attendants try to keep meal expenses to an absolute minimum since extra per diem means extra income.**

## Monthly Minimum Guarantee

As described in the Scheduling/Job Flexibility section, you can expect to "sit" reserve for most, if not all, of your first year as a flight attendant - and possibly longer depending on how quickly you gain seniority. With this in mind, consider the fact that reserves do not have set schedules and only earn flight time when lineholders are unable to fly. This creates an interesting situation with regard to monthly pay. You may be wondering what happens to your compensation during certain months when you work relatively few hours. Does the airline let you starve to death? Not quite. In these cases, you are paid what is called a *monthly minimum guarantee.*

This is a "safety net" that guarantees you will be paid for a set number of flight hours regardless of how little you actually fly in a given month. You are paid this amount even if you end up sitting home all month and do not fly a single trip. Should you exceed the monthly minimum (called *breaking guarantee*) you would no longer need the monthly minimum guarantee and would earn additional money for the extra hours flown.

Back to our Orion Airlines example. Let's say the minimum guarantee provided in the Orion Airlines contract is 71 hours. If you were to fly less than 71 hours in a given month, you would be paid: $19.05 x 71 =

$1,352.55 (minimum guarantee). Let's say you fly about 50 hours during the month, which requires you to be away from home for approximately 150 hours. You would be paid: $1.90 x 150 = $285.00 for meal expenses. This, added to your flight pay of $1,352.55, would bring your total monthly income to $1,637.55, or about $456 shy of earnings for a full month. Obviously, you would be earning less, but you would be working a lot less as well. If you only flew 50 hours a month for an entire year, you would earn: $1,637.55 x 12 = $19,650.60.

## Additional Income

Beyond the hourly base rate and per diem rate, there are many other ways to make money as a flight attendant. For example, if you are the lead flight attendant or a language speaker (LOD/O) during a given trip, you will usually receive additional pay - typically an extra $1.50 to $2.00 per hour. Flight attendants who work international flights are also often paid a higher rate.

Many airlines also pay premium rates to flight attendants who work at certain "less desirable" times of the day, week or year. For example, flight attendants who work at night or on certain weekends and holidays are typically paid a premium rate. At some airlines, flight attendants who work certain holidays are paid a rate equal to time and a half. At Orion Airlines, this would mean your hourly rate would jump from $19.05/hr to $28.58/hr!

From a scheduling standpoint, you are also sometimes allowed to earn extra money by flying more than the legal monthly flight hour limit. This is sometimes referred to as being on a *flight hour option*. You could elect, for example, to be on a 95-hour or 105-hour option. At Orion

Airlines, this could mean an extra $191 to $381 per month - not counting per diem

 **A senior international flight attendant at one of the big three major airlines, working maximum allowable hours with over 25 years of experience can earn over $100,000 per year!**

If you are real ambitious, you could also earn additional income by getting a management position as a supervisor, instructor, or interviewer. You could also consider a union-related position. Most of these positions will compensate you with a flat salary or credit you with more flight hours than a regular lineholder (e.g., 105 hours versus 85 hours), which equates to higher pay.

Also associated with pay is the income you may receive from any profit-sharing or stock option programs offered by your specific airline, not to mention the monetary value of the travel benefits you will receive.

# 6 BENEFITS

## Medical and Dental

Every major and most smaller airlines offer complete medical and dental coverage for all flight attendants, their spouses, and dependents. Some plans are better than others; the major airlines tend to offer the best, most extensive coverage.

 **Be sure to avoid airlines that do not provide at least some level of healthcare.**

Airlines usually offer medical and dental coverage through *health maintenance organizations* (HMOs) and *indemnity plans*. HMOs require you to choose a *primary care provider* from a limited network of participating physicians and hospitals. Every time you need to see a doctor, you are limited to your primary care provider; no coverage is provided should you schedule an appointment with any other physician. For every office visit, you pay a small co-payment, typically around $25 to $40 for 100% coverage. Routine physicals, prescriptions drugs, etc. are usually covered under the plan as well. In the more traditional fee-for-service indemnity plans, you do not have a primary care provider and, consequently, have the freedom to select any health care provider you wish, without limitation. Of course, this freedom does not come without a price. For every medical expense you incur, you must pay the entire fee out-of-pocket, fill out a claim form, and wait to get reimbursed by the insurance company. The level of reimbursement is usually 70 to 90%. Both HMOs and indemnity plans usually require regular monthly payroll deductions.

**Many HMOs have come under fire recently since patients cannot seek the help of medical specialists directly; an authorized referral from the primary care provider is required. HMOs claim to solve this problem, and save "everyone" money, by limiting the number of nonessential appointments with medical specialists. Of course, certain doctors may be hesitant to refer patients to specialists - even when necessary - because it costs the plan money, which potentially jeopardizes the doctor's membership in the plan. Nevertheless, recent data suggests that most HMO members - including flight attendants - are satisfied with their level of coverage.**

## Life Insurance

Most airlines offer group life insurance plans to all flight attendants who successfully complete initial training. These plans are either funded entirely by the airline or require you to pay a small monthly fee.

In most cases, you can increase the amount of your life insurance coverage (with certain limitations) by paying a monthly premium. Check with each airline for specific life insurance information.

## 401(k) and Defined Contribution Retirement Plans

Every major and most smaller airlines offer 401(k) programs that allow flight attendants to contribute a percentage of their pay to a self-directed, tax-free, retirement account each year. These funds can be invested in a variety of financial products, such as company stock or mutual funds.

Any financial advisor will tell you that enrollment in your company's 401(k) plan is the best way to plan for retirement. After all, your financial gains will accumulate tax-free until you are allowed to withdraw it after you are 59 1/2 years old. Plus, all money contributed to your 401(k) plan is exempt from income tax and is thus excluded from earned income reported on your W-2 form; it is as though you never earned the money! This could reduce your tax bracket and annual tax liability. Of course, once you begin withdrawing the money, you will be required to pay taxes on it. This typically occurs when you reach the age of 70 ½ when the IRS requires that you begin taking Minimum Required Distributions.(MRDs).

Some airlines also offer an employee 401(k) matching program in which they match your contributions in whole or in part up to a certain annual percentage. For example, if you contribute $4,000 to your 401(k) in a given year, and your airline offers an 8% match, your account would grow to $4,320 - irrespective of your investment performance from company stock and/or mutual funds.

A Defined Contribution Plan (or DC Plan) is another form of retirement funding offered by several airlines. The airline simply deposits a percentage of your earnings into a tax deferred fund and, like the 401k plan, offers you investment options. DC Plan funds are typically deposited into your account on a monthly basis.

**The maximum employee allowable contribution to a 401(k) plan is currently $18,500. Catch-up contributions for those 50 or older adds another $6,000. This does not include employer matching.**

## Profit-Sharing

During contract negotiations, union representatives and airline management sometimes settle their differences by establishing employee profit-sharing plans. In exchange for employee concessions (e.g., increased productivity, modified work rules, and pay caps), management typically offers a certain percentage of its annual net operating profits for distribution among employees. Under profit-sharing plans, employees benefit when the airline is making money, but have no benefit during industry downturns or unprofitable periods.

**In 2018, Southwest distributed a $543 million profit sharing payment to all of its employees due to another profitable year. That's the equivalent of about five weeks pay per employee!**

Not all airlines offer profit sharing, and you should keep in mind that even those that do offer profit sharing plans may not continue to do so for very long. As each new flight attendant contract is negotiated, features from the previous contract are subject to change.

## Stock Options

Some airlines issue company stock to their employees - including flight attendants - in the form of stock options at specified times of the year.

A stock option is a contract that gives you the right to purchase company stock at a discount. As a flight attendant that has been awarded stock options, you have the **option** to buy company stock at a discounted price at some point in the future (i.e., after a specific exercisable date). In short, if the stock goes up and you have held onto your options long enough (beyond the exercisable date), you can buy the stock at a discount (called *exercising your option*) and sell it the same day for an immediate profit.

For example, let's say your airline has a stock option program that issues 100 options of its common stock on January 1st of each year at $50 per share, and the plan requires you to hold onto these options for a minimum of one year before exercising on them. The options are deposited by the company into a brokerage account until you decide what you would like to do with them. One year later, the stock price grows to $100 per share. This means you could purchase the stock at the discounted price of $50 per share and sell it the same day at $100 per share. You would realize $50 profit for each share of stock you own, which is equal to $5,000 (less tax). If, on the other hand, your company stock price went to $25 per share, your options would be worthless. You could also choose to exercise your options and not sell them, meaning you would just purchase the 100 shares of stock at $50 per share.

Options are an excellent source of additional income and a good way to accumulate company stock, especially if the stock price is climbing and the airline has a good track record for increasing shareholder equity.

 **During bear markets and bad economic times, stock options are not even worth the paper they are written on. So, be careful in choosing an airline that pays less than the industry standard, but makes exaggerated promises about its stock option program.**

## Sick Time

In general, flight attendants accrue sick time for every month they work, usually between 4 and 5 hours per month. Sick time accumulates in a *sick bank*, which can be drawn from in the event of illness.

You are charged for sick time every time you are unable to fly a scheduled trip. For example, if you are scheduled to fly an 18-hour trip, but call in sick, 18 flight hours will be drawn from your sick bank. You, as well as the reserve called in to replace you, will be fully compensated for the 18-hour trip. As a result, the company sometimes pays two people to fly a single trip - one to sit home sick and the other to work the trip.

 **In some cases, depending on the size of your sick bank, you may be able to take an extended sick leave for several months without missing a paycheck.**

Because of the liberal nature of the system, it can be very tempting to frequently call in sick. After all, if you want to take a weekend off, you can just call in sick - assuming you have sufficient sick time in your sick bank. To combat this temptation, many airlines have begun to require doctor's notices from "sick" flight attendants, especially those with poor attendance records. Other airlines, to discourage abusive practices, have begun to offer incentives for exemplary attendance records, such as bonuses or positive-space travel privileges.

For those on extended sick leave with serious medical problems, some airlines offer a system that allows for the rapid re-accrual of sick time (2 to 3 times the normal rate) upon the flight attendant's return to duty. The reason for this is to rapidly rebuild an exhausted sick bank due to long-term disability.

## Leaves of Absence

Leaves of absence are becoming more and more common among flight attendants as they are increasingly pursuing interests outside of their profession.

Airlines grant leaves of absence based on their particular staffing needs at the time of the request. If an airline is in a high growth mode, it grants leaves of absence more readily than if it is in a maintenance or low growth mode.

Leaves of absence may be granted for any number of reasons; common leaves include maternity, education, and military leaves. The major advantage to taking a leave of absence is that you will continue to gain seniority while you are away. The downside is that your pay and benefits generally will be suspended until you return to work.

**Concerned about pregnancy? Most airlines are very sensitive to the needs of pregnant employees. During pregnancy, you have several options. You can take a formal maternity leave (lasting several months). Of course, this can put a large dent in your wallet, since virtually no airlines offer paid maternity leave. You can also manufacture your own paid maternity leave by using accrued sick time. If you are especially concerned about losing pay or sick time, some airlines may even assign you a temporary "desk job" after the 6th to 8th month of pregnancy. This way, you can work a bit longer without having to use unnecessary leave time. As you can see, you have quite a few options. Just be sure not to discuss pregnancy during the interview process and try to avoid going into labor during the probationary period. Airlines tend to be a lot less understanding about pregnancy when it comes to new-hires - plus you will have virtually no sick time to burn.**

## Vacations

Vacations at most airlines are awarded based on seniority. Flight attendants with the highest seniority are awarded the most vacation days during the most desirable times of year.

Vacations are bid on just like monthly lines of time; the most senior flight attendants receive their first choices, while those less senior receive less appealing alternatives. So, if you are at the bottom of the seniority totem pole, do not expect to be awarded a vacation during the summer months or over the Christmas holidays! These are very senior vacation periods.

With regard to pay, some airlines will pay you for trips missed, meaning that if you are scheduled to fly during your vacation, you will be paid for the entire trip. Other airlines will pay you for a flat number of hours for each vacation day taken (typically 4 to 5 hours per day) and will not pay you for trips missed. Others use a combination of both. In all cases, paid vacation hours reduce the total number of hours you will need to work (during your vacation month) to get your time in.

Many flight attendants strategically schedule their days off around vacation periods, essentially building "super-vacations." It is not uncommon for a senior flight attendant to parlay a 7-day vacation into 21 days off or longer, depending on the schedule. It is also possible, with some advanced planning, for a senior flight attendant to be on vacation for a week or more every other month (6 months per year) while only using 30 vacation days!

## Travel Privileges

Every airline offers its employees extensive travel benefits, including discounted or free space-available travel privileges to any one of its destinations, as well as discounts on other airlines that have reciprocal agreements.

The cost for travel varies from airline to airline, but most do not charge a fee for travel, except for international travel where taxes and entry fees may be imposed. Some airlines charge a flat fee for the entire year and offer unlimited travel privileges at no additional cost - with the exception of first class upgrades. In addition, most reciprocal agreements with other airlines allow you to travel at up to 90% off the highest coach fare or a flat fee.

Airlines vary on the extension of privileges, but most cover spouses, dependents, and parents. Most airlines also offer a certain number of space-available *companion* or *buddy passes* for friends and relatives outside your immediate family. Policies vary from airline to airline, but are generally very liberal.

The only drawback to space-available (or non-revenue) travel is that many flights are over-sold, especially those to popular destinations. So, a great deal of advanced planning is required on your part checking bookings, equipment type, frequency, etc. In some instances, it makes more sense to simply buy full-fare, positive-space tickets, especially if you are traveling with your family. This prevents you from getting *bumped* (i.e., removed from the airplane) in favor of paying passengers. It also prevents you from having to split-up your family among scattered, space-available seat assignments. After all, most people like to sit together when traveling.

**No matter how oversold an airplane may be, you can usually reach your destination by riding the flight attendant jump seat. The jump seat is an additional flight attendant seat located in the cabin on certain aircraft that is commonly used by flight attendants who commute to work. It is not the most comfortable seat onboard, but it serves its purpose.**

**If two employees attempt to book the same jump seat, it is generally awarded on a first come, first serve basis.**

There are many other travel-related benefits offered to airline employees. These include substantial discounts at hotels and resorts, plus cruise line, restaurant, airport gift shop, and car rental discounts. These are collectively known as *interline* discounts.

**If you want to learn more about interline discounts, type the word "interline" into any search engine. This will give you an idea of the many benefits available to airline employees. Keep in mind, these benefits are not just limited to travel. For example, depending on your airline agreement, you will typically receive up to 75% off at FedEx for all of your personal shipping needs.**

## Credit Unions

Every major and some smaller airlines have federal credit unions, which offer employees a variety of financial services. Some of these offer checking and savings accounts, direct payroll deposit services, and mortgage and auto loans.

Credit unions are generally employee-owned and although membership is completely voluntary, they do offer extremely competitive rates.

# 7 DUTIES AND RESPONSIBILITIES

## Preparing for the Trip

As described in the Scheduling/Job Flexibility section, you will probably begin your flight attendant career sitting reserve, living in a strange city, far away from what you now call home. During your on-duty days (roughly 19 days per month), you will be on call 24 hours a day. This will require you to carry a cell phone - unless, of course, you want to stay home all day (essentially on "house arrest") waiting for a phone call that may never come.

 **Make sure you choose a reliable cell phone provider with a large coverage area, since missing a quick call can cost you your job.**

Preparation for your trip begins long before the phone rings. As a new-hire, you will need to be packed and ready to go as soon as your on-duty period begins. After all, you may be contacted by crew scheduling for a trip that departs in under an hour, and that is certainly not the time to begin thinking about what you are going to pack for the trip. Most conscientious reserves will peruse the flight schedule before going on-duty so they can anticipate all possible destinations and climates. If it looks like they could be heading down south, they will pack their shorts and sneakers.

In addition to packing, it is necessary to have your uniform pressed, laid out, and ready to go before going on-duty. Furthermore, if your base has a lot of early departures on the schedule, you may need to shower and do your hair the night before. If you need money, do not put off going to the ATM. If your dog has to be brought to the kennel, you must make those arrangements ahead of time. If you have a spouse or any children, instructions need to be left for them. Many of the things you would normally do at home for yourself or for your family have to be delegated to others, such as buying groceries, writing bills, canceling appointments, etc.

Keep in mind, part of being prepared for a trip means not wandering great distances from your home. You can live your life and conduct normal day-to-day activities (with your cell phone in hand), but you should not go visit Aunt Harriet who lives 2 hours away or go on a 6-hour whale watch. Again, being late for check-in, especially while on probation, is not conducive to longevity with an airline!

As you gain seniority with an airline, the tasks associated with preparing for a trip will become second nature. For example, when you become a lineholder, you will have a regular schedule and know when and where you will be flying, when and what to pack, and what chores need to get done.

## Sick Calls

At some point during your career, chances are you will come down with the flu or some other illness while on duty. Your loyalty to the airline might make you inclined to go to work anyway, but this is not advisable; the airline would rather you stay home than spread the disease to 3 or 4 other crewmembers.

**You should never be afraid to call in sick. Of course, do not make a habit of calling in sick or you will earn a bad reputation with your supervisor (and eventually lose your job).**

When you are called to report to a trip that you are too sick to fly, you will need to tell crew scheduling that you are unable to work due to illness. They will take you off the trip and pass the information along to your supervisor; you should then contact your supervisor as well. In most cases, you will be paid for the trip and someone else will fly it for you.

Another situation you will likely experience during your career is the need to get off a trip due to illness. The same procedure above applies, but you will need to contact your supervisor first, then advise crew scheduling that you need to get off the trip, either coming through base or at a convenient location from which you can deadhead home. Your supervisor will most likely need a written report and require you to go to a hospital emergency room to be evaluated once you return to base. Again, you will be replaced and paid for the remainder of the trip.

## Getting to the Airport

When you are newly assigned to your initial domicile, you will probably be unfamiliar with the geography of the area. Because of this, you will need to get yourself well acquainted with one thing - how to get to the airport. Whether you are driving in your own car or using public transportation, do not wait until your first trip to try to figure this out, because if you get lost, you will be late to check-in and jeopardize your job.

The best way to learn how to get to the airport is to ask fellow employees. If you are driving, there are usually shortcuts that employees use to avoid traffic, and it would be very wise of you to find out about these as soon as possible.

**Use a reliable GPS, Google Maps or Waze on your smart phone. Or, get yourself a good map and highlight the route to the airport. Then, go out and drive it. You should do this several times during different times of the day, including rush hour. This will help you accurately determine how much time to allow to get to the airport.**

If there is a remote parking facility, you should know what the average travel time is from the parking lot to the terminal. Very often you will have to build additional time into your "time allowance" for waiting for the bus or van to pick you up. Once you have a number in your head on how long it will take you from your home to the terminal, add another half-hour for variables such as traffic, accidents, and detours; on bad weather days, add an hour.

Senior flight attendants know what types of traffic they will likely encounter at different times of the day. For this reason, they usually bid their trips around commuter traffic, either opting for very early or very late check-in times. As you gain seniority, you will become very comfortable with your commute, knowing exactly how much time to allow to get to the airport.

## Check-In

One of the first things you will learn how to do at your new crew base is find the *crew room*. This is the first place you will go upon reaching the terminal to check-in for a trip. It is here you will meet the other members of the flight crew you will be working with - specifically the pilots and other flight attendants. In the crew room, you will be required to check-in at one of the crew computer terminals.

Every pilot and flight attendant of a working flight crew must check-in within a certain amount of time of the departure time of their trip's first flight. Check-in time can vary from 1 to 3 hours, depending on whether it is a domestic or international trip; most domestic trips require you to check-in 1 hour prior to departure. At some airlines, you will work with the same crew (including pilots) for an entire trip, while at others, the cabin and cockpit crews will be on different schedules. So, in some cases, only flight attendants will check-in for a particular trip (the pilots will already be on the trip).

Check-in is a computerized system that allows crew schedulers to account for every member of the crew. When a crewmember checks-in at one of the computer terminals, the daily crew schedulers are immediately alerted that he or she is physically in the crew room and in position for the start of the trip. If check-in time passes, and all members of the crew have not checked-in, the crew schedulers will attempt to contact the missing person at the phone number on file with the company. If there is no answer, that person will be replaced. If you ever miss check-in without a good reason, you will have to answer to your supervisor.

Check-in is not just for "check-in." It is also an important time to tie up any administrative loose ends. For example, many flight attendants will discuss their position preferences for the trip during check-in; if you are assigned the senior flight attendant position and would rather work coach than first class, you would have the opportunity to swap positions with one of the flight attendants working the back.

Since the crew room is usually located adjacent to the crew mail room and supervisors' offices, check-in is also a good time to check your company mailbox, discuss issues with your supervisors, or just drop in to say, "hello."

## Crew Briefings

On the first leg of every trip, or upon meeting the cockpit crew for the first time, the captain will conduct a short crew briefing. The briefing, which is usually held in the cabin prior to passenger boarding, gives the captain an opportunity to exchange introductions with the first officer and cabin crew. It also allows him to go over some of the more important items relating to the flight. Some of the elements normally covered in a crew briefing are:

- Anticipated Flight time.
- Enroute and destination weather.
- Taxi time and ATC delays.
- Emergency and evacuation procedures.
- Medical emergency procedures.

- Cockpit entry procedures.
- Seat belt sign management and announcement procedures.
- Cockpit communication procedures.
- The handling of unruly or disruptive passengers.
- Carry-on luggage limitations.
- Passenger count information for the cockpit crew.
- Overwater briefing (if applicable).

At some point before or after the captain's briefing, the senior flight attendant will also conduct a crew briefing exclusively with the flight attendants. This normally involves:

- Relaying captain's information (e.g., estimated flight time, anticipated turbulence, weather, etc.).
- Determining who will make the PA announcements.
- Determining who will screen and brief the exit rows.
- Reviewing normal and emergency door operation for the specific aircraft.
- Making sure each flight attendant has an up-to-date emergency manual.
- Reviewing emergency procedures.
- Reviewing new procedures or revisions.

## In-Flight Duties

It may surprise you that the majority of flight attendant applicants do not understand the basic duties and responsibilities of the position. In fact, during the interview process, one of the most commonly asked questions - "What's a flight attendant's primary job responsibility?" - is often answered incorrectly.

# IS A FLIGHT ATTENDANT CAREER RIGHT FOR YOU?

 **Your primary duty as a flight attendant is to provide for the safety and comfort of all passengers onboard your flight!**

Overall, the flight attendant position involves performing a wide range of safety and customer service-related duties. In emergency situations, flight attendants must be prepared to provide direction and assistance for both passengers and the cockpit crew in accordance with government and company regulations. In non-emergency situations, flight attendants are responsible for providing the highest level of customer service to all customers; this means always performing your duties in a courteous and professional manner.

Some of the most common flight attendant duties include*:

- Pushing/pulling a 200+ pound beverage cart.
- Serving drinks and/or meals to passengers aboard the aircraft.
- Maintaining a comfortable temperature in the cabin by advising the cockpit crew of any passenger discomfort.
- Communicating with the cockpit crew in accordance with company policy about any abnormal sights, sounds or situations relating to the aircraft.
- Communicating with the cockpit crew in accordance with company policy about any passenger problems including unruly passengers, medical emergencies, distressed passengers or potential hijackings.
- Keeping passengers seated and belted during periods of turbulence and adverse weather.
- Hearing and interpreting the onboard chime system, determining its origin, and responding accordingly.

- Performing mathematical calculations that are required to complete inventory sheets, convert foreign currency, count meals, provide change from in-flight sales, and verify passenger headcount.
- Using and converting the 24-hour clock for yourself and passengers (e.g., a connecting flight that departs at 13:05, departs at 1:05 pm).
- Using and converting the 3-letter airport codes for yourself and passengers (e.g., ICT is the airport code for Wichita, Kansas).
- Handling unaccompanied minors.
- Operating exits in manual and emergency mode requiring two-handed gripping, rotating and pushing of door handles and operating doors weighing up to 70 pounds.
- Assisting disabled passengers during the flight by transporting them in the in-flight wheelchair, assisting with food handling, and conducting individual safety briefings.
- Reading announcements effortlessly without prior review.
- Assessing situations quickly to determine whether to initiate emergency evacuation procedures.
- Manipulating latches, switches, knobs and controls located throughout the aircraft.
- Handling emergency medical situations including administering emergency oxygen, CPR and/or using an onboard defibrillator.
- Memorizing and knowing the location of all emergency equipment onboard each aircraft and methodically performing procedures to operate emergency equipment when necessary.
- Being prepared to evacuate a full aircraft in less than 90 seconds if necessary.
- Being able to jump onto and slide down an inflated slide.

# IS A FLIGHT ATTENDANT CAREER RIGHT FOR YOU?

 Before interviewing with an airline, carefully review this section on flight attendant duties. Many interview questions are designed to assess your ability to carry out these duties. As a result, your knowledge of these duties will help you immensely during the interview process.

## Wheelchairs/Medical

Every airline is required by law to provide wheelchair access for disabled passengers. This means having a wheelchair and/or straightback (if required) to transport disabled passengers from the boarding area to their assigned seats on the airplane. Usually the wheelchair passengers are boarded first (before regular passengers) and deplaned last. Although a passenger service agent or other company representative will usually be responsible for boarding or deplaning wheelchair passengers, it is common on full flights (with multiple disabled persons) for flight attendants to assume this role.

 Handling wheelchair passengers adds a great deal of time to the boarding process. Winter "snowbird" flights to destinations such as West Palm Beach, Ft. Lauderdale, or Fort Myers, can sometimes have as many as 15 to 20 wheelchair passengers!

In addition to your duties relating to wheelchair passengers, you will also be trained to handle just about every possible medical emergency that can occur onboard an airplane. This will include the more routine problems that may require basic assistance, like handling airsickness, administering oxygen, and bandaging minor cuts and bruises. In addition, you will occasionally have to handle medical emergencies of a more serious nature, such as heart attacks, seizures, or loss of consciousness. During initial training, you will be trained in basic first aid, CPR, and how to use of the onboard defibrillator. To assist you in your medical duties, there are onboard first aid and medical kits containing drugs and medical supplies, such as bandages and splints. Certain medical kits may only be opened and used by medical practitioners, such as a RN, LPN or physician.

For airborne medical emergencies, aircraft are now capable of communicating directly with a professional medical facility and on-duty physician. One medical network known as *Medlink* allows for direct communication between the doctor and flight crew on how to handle a particular medical emergency. Some aircraft communicate via the cockpit radio, while others have a direct line to Medlink via the in-flight passenger telephone system. In any case, between your basic medical training and the guidance you will receive from Medlink, you should be well prepared to handle any type of medical emergency. This will allow you to direct the cockpit crew concerning the need to continue the flight or to divert for the safety of the passenger with the medical problem.

Another type of medical issue concerns the transport of human organs. Sometimes you will be asked to transport a human heart or human eyeballs to a medical recipient awaiting delivery for transplant surgery. These organs, usually packed in a special solution surrounded by dry ice inside a Styrofoam container, require that your aircraft be dispatched as a special *Lifeguard flight*. Although the captain should already be advised, you should confirm the Lifeguard status with the cockpit so they can advise Air Traffic Control of their call sign for preferential routing ahead of other traffic.

Another non-emergency medical issue that you will confront as a flight attendant concerns the boarding of special meals for passengers. These meals are specially ordered by passengers and can be necessary for a variety of reasons. Perhaps a passenger is on a salt-free diet for medical reasons, can only eat a vegetarian meal, or is a diabetic? There are also cases where all peanuts must be removed from an airplane due to a rare disease that makes people intolerant of the smell or taste of peanuts. Whatever the case, the senior flight attendant must be notified concerning the details of these meals and ensure they are boarded before departure. Failure to do so could jeopardize the health of these passengers.

## Unaccompanied Minors

Many people are unaware of the fact that there are many underage children out there accumulating a great deal of frequent flyer mileage. These children, usually the offspring of divorced parents, frequently travel by themselves to visit family members. These children are called *unaccompanied minors* or *unaccs* (pronounced "you-nacks"). Although there may be age variances between airlines for categorizing "unaccompanied" minors, the concept is the same. An underage child must be identified with a badge or identifying sticker and must be escorted on and off the airplane by a company representative until safely in the hands of the parent or guardian at the final destination. This is usually the responsibility of the senior flight attendant or his or her designee.

Although you will be well trained in handling unaccompanied minors, you should be aware that there are some potential pitfalls when dealing with children. For example, it is fairly common for an unaccompanied minor to try to "escape" from the airplane upon arrival. Keep in mind that the airline assumes a tremendous liability when transporting these minors and if a child is lost, the airline will be held accountable. Needless to say, if this happens on your watch, your job will be in jeopardy.

## Initial and Recurrent Training

Do not be intimidated by the above list of flight attendant duties. Although it may seem a bit overwhelming at first, you will be thoroughly trained in all these areas during your 4 to 7 weeks of initial training and every year at recurrent (also called refresher) training. During these training sessions, you will undergo an intensive training program covering an initial indoctrination on pay, benefits, uniforms, domiciles etc., along with the normal duties of a flight attendant, such as serving meals, doing PA announcements, learning aircraft equipment, 3-letter airport codes, etc. In addition, you will be required to actively participate in simulated emergency situations and operate emergency equipment on all aircraft types. Theses simulations are based on the possibility of actual scenarios, including evacuations, hijackings, bomb threats, fire-fighting, decompression, and hazardous material handling.

**Do not expect a 5-day "school week" with normal hours during your initial training; training sessions often occur on nights and weekends. And yes, you will be tested and tested again. Typically, you will need to score a minimum of 90% on all tests; one or two failures could spell your doom, depending on the airline.**

As mentioned above, initial training is generally 4 to 7 weeks, depending on the airline and is usually conducted in the corporate or operational home of the carrier. Other notables about initial training:

- Out of town trainees typically receive free airfare and lodging.
- Transportation is provided to and from the training facility; meals are also provided.
- Generally, there is no salary or benefits during training and employment is contingent upon the successful completion of the program.
- You can expect to have a same-gender roommate during training.

Paid refresher training (also called recurrent training) is normally conducted once a year for 1 to 2 days. The Federal Aviation Administration (FAA) requires that every flight attendant (at every airline) receive this training once per year; it is the law.

# 8 DOMICILES AND RELOCATION

## What's a Domicile?

According to Webster's dictionary, a domicile is "a dwelling place; a place of residence; a home." In the aviation world, the term *domicile* refers to your home base station, specifically the airport from which you will begin and end every trip.

Flight attendants commonly ask one other, "Where are you based?" or "What's your domicile?" Sample domiciles include Boston (BOS), Cleveland (CLE), and Los Angeles (LAX). Each domicile can be described using its 3-letter airport code. For example, a flight attendant based in Washington. D.C. can refer to his or her domicile as DCA (Washington National Airport).

Each airline has its own *limited* number of domiciles, typically in the range of 1 to 20. So, if you have ambitions of someday living in Los Angeles, for example, it will probably make sense to pick an airline with an LAX domicile.

Unless you plan on commuting, you will need to live in or near the city of your domicile assignment. This can be a nightmare if your airline bases you in a less-desirable city. With increased seniority, however, you will eventually be able to choose your own domicile.

## Initial Domicile Assignment

At some point during new-hire training, you will be given the opportunity to complete a domicile "dream sheet," specifying, in order of preference, where you would like to begin your career as a flight attendant. Domicile assignments are almost always awarded based on seniority. During new-hire training, initial seniority is usually determined by age, meaning the oldest members of the class will often get the best domicile assignments. However, airlines usually award domiciles based on the needs of the company. So, even if you are the most senior person in the class, you may not get your first choice. After all, there may not be any openings at your preferred base(s), and the airline may have more serious staffing needs at other, possibly less desirable ones.

Initial domicile assignment is very important to some people. Although one of the minimum hiring requirements at just about every airline is a willingness to relocate, many people are not willing to do so. It is common for a limited number of flight attendants to drop out of new-hire training simply because they do not receive their preferred domicile assignment. If initial domicile assignment is of critical importance to you, you may want to consider another profession.

## Choosing a Domicile

So, there you are in class, and the day comes to fill out your list of preferred domiciles. The problem is, you are from East Podunk and have no idea what life is like in the domicile cities your airline offers. What do you do?

There are many factors to consider when choosing an initial domicile, including domicile size, cost-of-living, accessibility, and base "personality." Although it is not always possible to select the "perfect" domicile, you can certainly come up with a few solid choices. You must realize, however, that there are always trade-offs involved when evaluating domiciles. For example, you may want to be based in New York because it is a very junior base (at a particular airline) and will allow you **to** become a regular lineholder in the least amount of time. What is the trade-off? The cost-of-living is extremely high.

- **Size** - The size of a base is important for a number of reasons. Since you will probably sit reserve during your early years as a flight attendant, you will only get the opportunity to fly when lineholders call in sick, become illegal, or are otherwise unable to work - and perhaps during holiday periods when *extra sections* are added to the flight schedule. Let's face it, these are unique situations, and at a small base, where there are obviously fewer flights than at a large base, reserve flight attendants will fly very little certain months. After all, fewer flights means fewer opportunities for reserves. And not flying means less pay, since you will probably only earn the minimum guarantee, not to mention receive little to no per diem. Also, a small base probably won't give you the necessary flying experience you will need to become entirely comfortable with your new career. In short, we strongly recommend choosing a large domicile.

- **Cost-of-living** - When considering a domicile, you should pay serious attention to cost-of-living statistics. As a reserve, most airlines require you to live within a certain driving distance from the airport (usually within 1 hour), so you should research every domicile city you are considering very carefully. For example, you may want to review average housing and grocery costs, local income tax rates, and other relevant information. Boston and New York are popular domiciles for many airlines. Although they may be exciting places to live, the cost-of-living in these cities is extremely high. Many flight attendants will opt for cities like these, however, and share expenses with other flight attendants. It is very common for reserves to live in a house or apartment with 5 or 6 other flight attendants in a high cost-of-living area! So, if living alone is important to you, you may want to choose a domicile that has a low cost-of-living.
- **Accessibility** - Accessibility refers to: 1) how accessible an airport is via automobile; 2) how accessible an airport is via airplane. First, let's consider driving accessibility. There are many elements to consider when evaluating an airport's driving accessibility. Is rush hour a nightmare? Can you live in close proximity to the airport or must you live an hour away? Will you be living near an airport that is in "the middle of nowhere" with nothing to occupy your time?

**Charlotte, NC is an example of a very accessible airport. There are many nice communities within 10 to 15 minutes of the airport and the drive is a pleasant one.**

Another issue to consider is how accessible the airport is by air. In other words, what type of route structure does the airline offer to and from your domicile city? This is important because once you become a lineholder with a regular schedule, you may want to consider relocating your primary residence, but stay based at your existing domicile; in other words, you may want to commute. Unfortunately, commuting is not an enjoyable experience, but many people choose this lifestyle due to the flexibility it offers. If you are based at a domicile which offers limited flight service or does not offer non-stop flight service to and from the city of your primary residence, commuting can make your life miserable. Another factor relating to air accessibility that you should consider is your travel privileges. Since you will probably be traveling using space-available passes on your days off, the more flights offered at a particular domicile, the better. For example, you will have a better chance of getting to Miami if you domicile offers hourly service as opposed to just 1 or 2 flights per day. some cities, with less-accessible airports, getting a non-revenue seat to any destination can be a great challenge; airplanes fill up with paying passengers. Most of the major hub airports, however, are very accessible by air.

- **Base "personality"** - Another important aspect to consider when choosing your initial domicile is the base "personality": what type of people are based there? Certain bases attract certain types of people. For example, northern bases attract northerners and southern bases attract southerners. Also, you should consider the attitude of the supervisors and the seniority of the base. Supervisors at some bases are very lenient while others run their operations like marine boot camps. With regard to seniority, if you choose a very senior base, you will sit reserve for a very long time. Ask around and you will be able to get a good feel for each base's unique personality.

## Domicile Transfer

So, you have been assigned to your new base and, after one month, you are miserable. The cost of living is too high; you like traveling to Fort Lauderdale to see your family, but flight service is too infrequent from your base; you do not like the people, and the supervisors are not very friendly. What do you do? You put in for a transfer!

Most airlines require you to remain at your base of initial assignment for a minimum period of time, typically 3 months to a year. After that, you are free to request a domicile transfer. Transfer assignments, like everything else in the airline business, are based on seniority. Once your transfer becomes effective, you may be given moving days to relocate - depending on the airline.

**If you receive a less-than-favorable domicile assignment during new-hire training, do not take it too hard. You can usually transfer to another base within a few short months, so it is certainly not a reason to quit!**

## Commuting

Many lineholding flight attendants choose domiciles that are located halfway across the country from their primary residence and commute to work. This is quite common for both flight attendants and pilots because of the ample number of days off between trips and the free or reduced-cost travel benefits. It is particularly common for a flight attendant to commute to work if his or her spouse must work in a particular part of the country

 **While you are a reserve, commuting is neither encouraged, nor practical. In some cases, it is not even allowed.**

There are many negative aspects to commuting. First of all, nobody truly enjoys commuting. With the passenger loads constantly increasing, commuters are always on edge as to whether or not they are going to make check-in. Consequently, most commuters depart for work hours earlier than necessary. That way, even if primary flights are delayed or cancelled, they will be able to make it to their domicile on time. In some cases, especially for trips with early departures, commuters must leave home the night before their trip and stay in a hotel or apartment to ensure they make it work on time the next day; it is common for commuters to share a commuter apartment (also called a *crash pad*) with 10 or 12 flight attendants for these types of situations (but it is seldom a "full house," due to varying schedules).

Although the upside of commuting is that you can live virtually anywhere in the country (or, in some cases, the world), the downside is that you will waste a lot of time and money in the process, not to mention shave years off your life because of the stress level of getting to work on time. After all, there is zero tolerance for tardiness in this profession and "commuting trouble" is not a valid excuse for being late to check-in.

## Employee Parking

All airlines provide flight attendants with employee parking at their domicile. The cost is covered by the airline and you are allowed to park your car in a designated employee parking facility at or nearby the airport. Usually there is some sort of van or bus service from the parking area to the terminal.

If you are a commuter, you will be required to pay for parking *out-of-pocket* at the airport which serves the area you live, but the company will provide free parking at your domicile - assuming you have a car there.

**If you decide to commute to work, you should realize that employee parking can be a significant expense, depending on where you live. For example, in Boston, employee parking can cost over $1,000 per year!**

# 9 MANAGEMENT OPPORTUNITIES

## Supervisors

Every flight attendant has a supervisor he or she must report to. In a small base, there may be only 2 or 3 supervisors handling the entire base; in a large base, there can be as many as 40 or 50 supervisors. Supervisory personnel generally receive greater pay than "regular" flights attendants who fly monthly lines of time; however, actual pay varies by airline and position (as well as other factors). Supervisors are considered a part of airline management and report directly to management personnel and department heads in the airline chain of command.

Supervisors are responsible for flight attendants in many ways. If you are out sick repeatedly, your supervisor may ask you for a detailed explanation of the problem or a written doctor's report. If you have a run-in with another flight attendant or are *written up* by an irate passenger, you will be called into your supervisor's office. Furthermore, if you wish to request a leave of absence, or have a work-related problem that needs to be addressed, you will need to talk to your supervisor.

**Supervisors sometimes show up unexpectedly on your flights to spot check your performance and ensure your adherence to company uniform and grooming guidelines.**

Supervisors are also very involved in the flight attendant hiring process. After you have gained at least 2 to 3 years of seniority with a particular airline, you may declare an interest in becoming a supervisor. The process is fairly simple: contact your supervisor, submit your resume, and interview for the position (along with many other applicants). Airline management usually looks for individuals with a supervisory background and a college or postgraduate degree.

If you think you would enjoy the challenge of working in a supervisory position and would prefer to work in an office and be home virtually every night - rather than fly the friendly skies - then a supervisory position might be for you.

**If you have ambitions of becoming a flight attendant supervisor someday, you should realize that this position does not require you to give up your flying duties entirely. Supervisors still get to fly occasionally; typically one trip per month.**

## Trainers/Instructors

Every airline has a training center where new-hire and recurrent training takes place. Staffing at these training facilities is usually very extensive, given the vast number of topics and procedures that need to be continually communicated to flight attendant personnel. Some trainers teach very specific subjects, while others instruct on a broad range of topics. Additionally, some flight attendants work exclusively with new-hire trainees, while others specialize in recurrent training. Most instructors begin their careers as flight attendants and are thus able to draw upon their own, real-world experience during training.

Trainers and instructors generally receive greater pay than flight attendants (with comparable experience) who fly regular lines of time. They must, however, relocate to the city of the airline training facility, which can be rather limiting. Their schedules offer quite a bit of variety; some days they teach classes, while other days they tend to administrative tasks. Occasionally, they even get to fly to other bases to conduct recurrent training.

If you think you would like the variety of the training environment and enjoy speaking in front of large groups of people, a position as a trainer could be for you. Of course, you will have to gain at least 2 to 3 years of seniority before you could even think of applying for this position.

## Interviewers

Some airlines use professional interviewers to hire flight attendants (usually members of the human resources department), while others use actual flight attendants to conduct interviews.

Some airlines use lineholding flight attendants to conduct interviews on an *as needed* or part-time basis. Lineholding flight attendants are used to conduct preliminary interviews and pre-screen prospective applicants. More advanced second and third interviews, as well as final hiring decisions, are usually handled by supervisors. Since it is a part-time position, these flight attendants typically fly regular lines of time and interview when needed. Compensation is usually in the form of a premium rate, but sometimes it is merely a reimbursement for missed flight hours.

## Departmental Positions

Every airline is made up of departments, such as flight operations, inflight services, scheduling, marketing, etc., and each department has a department head who oversees the entire business unit. In addition to the department head position, there are also numerous middle management positions available within each department Some departmental positions are filled from within the airline, while others are the result of outside recruitment. Competition is fierce for these highly coveted positions and a college degree is usually required.

If you think you might be interested in becoming a part of the management team someday, you should check with each airline for minimum qualifications and hiring practices. After all, you want to make sure your future employer would consider promoting a senior flight attendant to such a position.

## Corporate Positions

Above the department heads, in the airline hierarchy, are the executives and corporate vice presidents who work directly for the President and Chief Executive Officer. Most airlines recruit outside the airline for these positions, but there have been rare instances where flight attendants were promoted to the executive ranks. Of course, these flight attendants had advanced degrees and exemplary resumes

# 10 FEAR FACTORS

## Fear of Flying

Although flying is an integral part of the job, ironically, many flight attendants are afraid to fly. They often start out okay, but as they mature, they usually begin to think about their loved ones and how they would fare in the event of a disaster.

Flight attendants who are afraid to fly cope with it in many different ways. Some ignore it, while others resort to counseling. The more serious cases usually result in temporary medical leaves until they are able to overcome (or suppress) their *aeroanxiety*.

 It is very normal to have a certain amount of "flight fright." So, do not let a diminutive fear of flying discourage you from pursuing a flight attendant career.

Obviously, this section is not designed to help you overcome a fear of flying, but there are many books on the market written by both airline personnel and psychologists that *can* help you. There are also courses you can take to overcome aerophobia. Most books and courses emphasize the industry's impressive safety record (as compared to other forms of transportation), thus suggesting aerophobia can be overcome just by educating yourself!

 2017 was the safest year in history for airline passengers worldwide.

## Turbulence

Turbulence is the leading cause of injury in non-fatal airline accidents. Since 2002, there have been more than 563 turbulence-related incidents resulting in serious bodily injury to passengers and crew as well as damage to aircraft. Unfortunately, because flight attendants are usually the last to be seated, they are most susceptible to injury.

# IS A FLIGHT ATTENDANT CAREER RIGHT FOR YOU?

 **A 150 to 200 pound rolling beverage cart in turbulent weather can result in serious personal injury or even death under the right circumstances.**

Pilots certainly attempt to avoid turbulence, but oftentimes, even the most skilled pilots cannot avoid a massive pocket of severely unstable air.

During a turbulent flight, the captain will brief the lead flight attendant on the severity of the situation and any special precautions that need to be taken to ensure the safety of all passengers and crew. Sometimes, during especially turbulent flights, the captain will ask that food and/or beverage service be suspended and for all flight attendants to take their seats.

Each year, a number of commercial jet aircraft are damaged due to atmospheric turbulence. But there is a larger issue involved, that of injury to passengers. Sadly, most turbulence-related injuries could be avoided if passengers simply fastened their seat belts. In 98% of cases, the injured parties were not wearing their seat belts at the time of injury, even though the "fasten seat belt" sign was ON. This is not only unsafe, but it is a federal violation.

The geographic distribution of reported incidents of turbulence tends to mirror predominant route structures and, to some extent, unstable weather patterns, with the heaviest concentration in southern and eastern sections of the United States.

As a flight attendant, you should be aware of the weather at all times; read the weather page of the USA Today and watch the Weather

Channel. Since most turbulence and low-level *windshear* are associated with bad weather (especially thunderstorms, hurricanes and tornadoes) you should pick your trips accordingly. For example, if you would like to schedule frequent layovers in West Palm Beach during the month of July, but see that thunderstorm activity is in the forecast, you might want to reconsider. Of course, if you are a reserve, you won't have this luxury. If you must go, be sure to get briefed by the captain. In addition, you will want to be firm with your passengers: they must wear their seatbelts when the "fasten seat belt" sign is active; it could save their lives! Of course, as you are trying to enforce that passengers wear their safety belts during turbulent conditions, you will put yourself at risk. But this is a necessary part of the job; your number one priority is passenger safety.

This section is not meant to alarm you or make you think that every time you fly you should expect a rough flight. In fact, anything greater than light *chop* is rare, and most of your flights will be as smooth as glass. But if you are prepared for the worst, then it will make your life easier when turbulence does creep up on you unexpectedly. The **Turbulence Chart** in the Appendix outlines the different types of air turbulence you might encounter.

## Disruptive Passengers (Air Rage)

No doubt you have heard of *road rage*, the term used to describe the actions of vengeful drivers who have turned the roadways into a modern-day battlefield. If you take "their" parking spaces, cut them off at intersections, or otherwise provoke them, you could end up with damage to your vehicle and/or personal injury.

Unfortunately, the same phenomenon is spreading to the world's airlines in the form of *air rage*. With an increasing number of flight delays, cancellations, and overcrowded airplanes, many passengers are unjustly venting their frustrations on airline employees through malevolent and violent acts.

Although this book is not designed to address the reasons for air rage, suffice it to say that it is becoming a very serious problem that has received a great deal of media attention.

Some passengers feel that when they walk onto an airplane, they have the right to verbally abuse, humiliate or even assault flight attendants (and pilots) in uniform. Although the corporate stance on this issue has always been that "the passenger is always right," airlines have begun to aggressively respond to the problem in defense of their flight crews. Many airlines have even installed a type of handcuff restraining device, called *tuff cuffs*, for restraining unruly passengers.

Many recent incidents have resulted in a growing number of private lawsuits between crewmembers and passengers. Some of these lawsuits have resulted in passengers serving prison time and/or paying severe fines.

**Interfering with the duties of a crewmember onboard a flight is a federal offense punishable by fine and/or imprisonment.**

As a flight attendant, you should be aware that air rage is a very real issue, but it absolutely should not dissuade you from pursuing a flight attendant career. A number of airlines, organizations, and government agencies, have finally begun to address and research the problem, which should result in improved working conditions for all crewmembers in the very near future. In the short-term, however, the more you understand the reasons for air rage, the more prepared you will be to deal with it. During your initial and recurrent training as a flight attendant, you will be taught specific techniques for dealing with disruptive passengers. This training should prepare you for just about every type of air rage disruption.

Many airlines have even installed a type of handcuff restraining device, called *tuff cuffs*, for restraining unruly passengers.

Many recent incidents have resulted in a growing number of private lawsuits between crewmembers and passengers. Some of these lawsuits have resulted in passengers serving prison time and/or paying severe fines.

# USEFUL LINKS

**AirlineCareer.com website**
http://airlinecareer.com

**Flight Attendant Free Online Prequalification Test**
http://airlinecareer.com/tests/flight-attendant-pre-qualification-test/

**Flight Attendant Jobs Blog**
http://airlinecareer.com/flight-attendant-jobs-blog/

**AirlineCareer.com Twitter Page**
http://twitter.com/airlinecareer

**AirlineCareer.com Facebook Page**
http://www.facebook.com/pages/AirlineCareercom/150859331603035

**Flight Attendant Career FAQs**
http://airlinecareer.com/about/faq/

**Flight Attendant Airport Codes Test**
http://airlinecareer.com/tests/airport-codes-test/

**Flight Attendant 24-Hour Clock Test**
http://airlinecareer.com/tests/24-hr-clock-test/

**Flight Attendant Hours and Minutes Test**
http://airlinecareer.com/tests/hours-and-minutes-test/

**Flight Attendant PA Announcements**
http://airlinecareer.com/tests/pa-announcements/

**Flight Attendant Dictionary**
http://airlinecareer.com/tests/flight-attendant-dictionary/

**How to Answer Flight Attendant Interview Questions**
http://airlinecareer.com/products/

**US Department of State (for Passports)**
https://Travel.State.gov

**Boeing Aircraft:**
http://www.boeing.com/commercial/products.html

**Airbus Aircraft:**
http://www.airbus.com/aircraftfamilies/passengeraircraft/

**Embraer Aircraft:**
http://www.embraercommercialjets.com/#/en/familia-ejets/1

# APPENDIX

## Sample Schedule – Regular Line of Time

Below is a sample schedule for Orion Airlines (fictitious airline). Bold text is for explanation only and will not appear in your line.

The schedule (line number 6014) features four 3-day trips during the month of December, plus a final trip that begins on the 31st and extends into January. The first trip (pairing #13053) begins on Sunday, December 3. It includes 2 RONs (Remain Overnight), requiring you to spend the night in Wilkes-Barre/Scranton on Sunday and Phoenix on Monday. The trip ends on Tuesday. This same trip (pairing #13053) is repeated on the 10th, 17th, and 24th and 31st. This schedule requires you to work 13 days for the month, but gives you 18 full days off. The major problem with this schedule is the RON in Wilkes-Barre/Scranton on Christmas eve and New Year's Eve, and Phoenix on Christmas day and New Year's Day - but working holidays is a part of the job (only senior flight attendants can successfully bid them off).

Most airlines will only pay you from the time an aircraft pushes back from the gate to the time it arrives at the gate of its destination; this is known as *flight time*, *block time*, or *hard time*. If you look toward the bottom of the schedule, you will notice that the total block time for the month is 79 hours and 57 minutes. You will also notice *pay time*, which is 79 hours and 57 minutes. Pay time includes block time plus any excess *claim time*. Claim time is time paid in excess of block time (e.g., time paid for deadheading, excessive on-duty time, etc.). In this example, there is no claim time, so pay time is equal to block time. Your base monthly salary is based on pay time.

So, if your base rate were $19.05/hr, you would earn a base monthly salary of $19.05/hr x 79 hrs and 57 min, which equals $1,523.05.

When analyzing a monthly line of time for bidding purposes, it is important to look at the associated *trip pairings* as well

## Regular Line of Time

|     |   | Dec-2017 |                                         |
|-----|---|----------|-----------------------------------------|
|     |   | 6014     | **Line Number**                         |
|     |   |          |                                         |
| 28L | T |          |                                         |
| 29L | W |          |                                         |
| 30L | T |          |                                         |
| 1   | F |          |                                         |
| 2   | S |          |                                         |
| 3   | S | 13053    | **1$^{st}$ Trip of month (Pairing 13053)** |
| 4   | M | AVP      |                                         |
| 5   | T | PHX      |                                         |
| 6   | W |          |                                         |
| 7   | T |          |                                         |
| 8   | F |          |                                         |
| 9   | S |          |                                         |
| 10  | S | 13053    | **2$^{nd}$ Trip of month**              |
| 11  | M | AVP      |                                         |
| 12  | T | PHX      |                                         |
| 13  | W |          |                                         |
| 14  | T |          |                                         |
| 15  | F |          |                                         |
| 16  | S |          |                                         |
| 17  | S | 13053    | **3$^{rd}$ Trip of month**              |

# IS A FLIGHT ATTENDANT CAREER RIGHT FOR YOU?

| 18 | M | AVP | |
|---|---|---|---|
| 19 | T | PHX | |
| 20 | W | | |
| 21 | T | | |
| 22 | F | | |
| 23 | S | | |
| 24 | S | 13053 | **4th Trip of month** |
| 25 | M | AVP | |
| 26 | T | PHX | |
| 27 | W | | |
| 28 | T | | |
| 29 | F | | |
| 30 | S | | |
| 31 | S | 13074 | **Final Trip of Month, extends into next month** |
| | | | |
| PAY | | 79:57 | **Pay Time for month** |
| NITE | | 15:18 | |
| DAY | | 64:39 | |
| BLK | | 79:57 | **Block Time for month** |
| LNDS | | 35 | **Landings for month** |
| DPS | | 13 | |
| DAYS | | 13 | **Workdays for month** |
| | | | |

## TRIP PAIRING #13053

Trip pairing #13053 is a 3-day trip (each day is referred to as a Duty Period). The first segment (also called a *leg*) of the trip involves departing Boston at 6:00 A.M. with scheduled arrival in Washington, D.C. at 7:36 A.M. The aircraft is a 737 and the flight number is 421. The Equipment type code is 3L. You would earn 1 hour and 36 minutes of block time for this first leg of the trip. After a 40 minute layover in Washington, D.C., Flight 421 will continue with service to Kansas City. After 2 more legs, Day #1 will end with a RON in Wilkes-Barre/Scranton at the Ramada Plaza Hotel; BRK stands for "Break" and is synonymous with RON. The total block time for Day #1 is 7 hours and 24 minutes. The total RON Time for Day #1 is 14 hours and 4 minutes. You can review the rest of the trip on your own. Be sure to note the duty time and pay time for each day and the totals at the base of the page.

## PAIRING# 13053     DUTY PERIOD#1
## DAILY EXCEPT WEDS DEC 6 & SUN DEC 31

|    | FLT | BLKT | L/O | CITIES & TIMES |
|----|-----|------|-----|----------------|
| 3L | 421 | 1+36 | n/a | BOS 600 716 DCA |
|    | 421 | 2+52 | +40 | DCA 816 1108 MCI |
| 3L | 331 | 2+00 | +37 | MCI 1145 1345 PIT |
| 34 | 820 | +56  | 2+45 | PIT 1630 1726 AVP |

DTY=12+41 BLK=7+24   DHD=+0   DRD=+0   MIN=+0

TCR=+0        PAY=7+24   BRK=14+04   S1   VM=6+00

RAMADA PLAZA HOTEL   717-824-7100

## IS A FLIGHT ATTENDANT CAREER RIGHT FOR YOU?

**PAIRING# 13053    DUTY PERIOD#2**

| | FLT | BLKT | L/O | CITIES & TIMES |
|---|---|---|---|---|
| 3L | 1211 | 1+03 | n/a | AVP 730  833 PIT |
| 34 | 155 | 4+43 | 1+22 | PIT 955  1438 PHX |

DTY=8+23  BLK=5+46   DHD=+0   DRD=+0   MIN=+0

TCR=+0        PAY=5+46    BRK=24+56   S1    VM=4+30

FAIRFIELD INN & SUITES   888-217-1426

**PAIRING# 13053    DUTY PERIOD#3**

| 3L | FLT | BLKT | L/O | CITIES & TIMES |
|---|---|---|---|---|
| | 164 | 4+27 | n/a | PHX 1534  2001 PHL |
| 34 | 2154 | 1+18 | 1+29 | PHL 2130  2248 BOS |

DTY=8+29  BLK=5+45   DHD=+0   DRD=+0   MIN=+0

TCR=+0        PAY=5+45    PRG=+0    S1    VM=4+30

TRIP=66+03 DAY=15+36 NIGHT=3+19   PAY=18+55

# Reserve Line of Time

Below is a sample schedule for Orion Airlines (fictitious airline). As a reserve, you can expect to have a schedule similar to this one.

|  |  | Dec-2017 |  |
|---|---|---|---|
|  |  | 4003 | Line Number |
|  |  |  |  |
| 1 | F | X | X denotes days off. All other days on duty. |
| 2 | S | X |  |
| 3 | S | X |  |
| 4 | M |  |  |
| 5 | T |  |  |
| 6 | W |  |  |
| 7 | T |  |  |
| 8 | F | X |  |
| 9 | S | X |  |
| 10 | S |  |  |
| 11 | M |  |  |
| 12 | T |  |  |
| 13 | W |  |  |
| 14 | T |  |  |
| 15 | F | X |  |
| 16 | S | X |  |
| 17 | S | X |  |
| 18 | M | X |  |
| 19 | T |  |  |

## IS A FLIGHT ATTENDANT CAREER RIGHT FOR YOU?

| 20 | W | | |
|----|---|---|---|
| 21 | T | | |
| 22 | F | | |
| 23 | S | | |
| 24 | S | X | |
| 25 | M | X | |
| 26 | T | | |
| 27 | W | | |
| 28 | T | | |
| 29 | F | | |
| 30 | S | | |
| 31 | S | | |
| | | | |

## Turbulence Chart

| Intensity | Aircraft Reaction | Reaction Inside Aircraft |
|---|---|---|
| **Light Turbulence (common)** | Momentary, slight erratic changes in altitude and/or attitude, or chop causing slight, rapid and somewhat rhythmic bumpiness without appreciable changes in altitude or attitude. | Slight strain against seat belts or shoulder harness. Unsecured objects may be displaced. Food service may be conducted and little or no difficulty encountered in walking. |
| **Moderate Turbulence (occasional)** | Turbulence similar to light, but greater intensity. Changes in altitude and/or attitude, but the aircraft remains under control at all times. Variation in airspeed, or Chop causing rapid bumps or jolts without appreciable changes in aircraft altitude or attitude. | Definite strain against seat belts or shoulder harness. Unsecured objects are dislodged. Food service and walking difficult. |

| Intensity | Aircraft Reaction | Reaction Inside Aircraft |
|---|---|---|
| **Severe Turbulence** (hardly ever) | Turbulence causing large abrupt changes in altitude and/or attitude. It usually causes variations in indicated airspeed. Aircraft may be momentarily out of control. | Forced violently against seat belts or shoulder harness. Unsecured objects are tossed about. Food service and walking are impossible. |
| **Extreme Turbulence** (almost never) | Aircraft is impossible to control. It may cause structural damage. | |

## ABOUT THE AUTHOR

Joseph Belotti is a captain for a major airline, a former US Navy pilot and a retired naval officer. Captain Belotti has been an airline industry veteran for over 40 years and has logged over 30,000 hours in his 49 year aviation career. He is a graduate of the College of the Holy Cross in Worcester, Massachusetts and holds an MBA degree from Western New England College in Wilbraham, Massachusetts. Captain Belotti is currently an Aircraft Delivery and Maintenance Test Pilot for JetBlue flying the Airbus A320 and A321 aircraft and is President and Founder of AirlineCareer.com, a website for aspiring flight attendants. He has served as an airline recruiter for both pilots and flight attendants and was a recruiter for the United States Naval Academy. Captain Belotti is also the author of "How to Answer Flight Attendant Interview Questions," the first book in the "How to Become a Flight Attendant" series.

## ABOUT THE PUBLISHER

AirlineCareer.com is dedicated to providing men and women of all ages and backgrounds the necessary resources to evaluate, pursue, and maintain successful flight attendant careers in the US and overseas. The site, with a member and registered user base of over 90,000 from all 50 states and 100 foreign countries, was created by a US major airline captain and flight attendant supervisors. It was launched in August, 2000 and offers individuals comprehensive information on career evaluation and step-by-step instruction on how to apply for and land a job with a major, national or regional airline. Recently, the site was recognized as one of the top aviation web sites by John A. Merry, author of 'The Aviation Internet Directory: A Guide to the 500 Best Web Sites,' published by Aviation Week/McGraw Hill.

## FINAL THOUGHTS

We hope you have learned a great deal from reading **"Is a Flight Attendant Career Right For You?"** Thank you again for your purchase. If you have time, we would appreciate it if you could post a review and share your experience with those who might be interested in our book. You may also want to check out the Kindle edition of this book which has the same material, but offers clickable links.

Please keep in mind that the information in this publication is only a fraction of the information we offer at Airlinecareer.com, a flight attendant career website that teaches you everything you need to know about getting an airline job.

We also publish a free weekly blog, Facebook™ and Twitter™ pages. Links to some of our services and other sites are listed on the Useful Links page. We also offer additional publications on a variety of subjects relating to the flight attendant career. Click here for more information.

We wish you luck in your flight attendant job search and hope to see you onboard again soon!

Best Regards,

Joseph P. Belotti, Jr.
President
AirlineCareer.com

# IS A FLIGHT ATTENDANT CAREER RIGHT FOR YOU?

www.ingramcontent.com/pod-product-compliance
Lightning Source LLC
Chambersburg PA
CBHW020444220526
45464CB00002B/854